The 13th Step

The 13th Step

A Global Journey in Search
of Our Cosmic Destiny

Jude Currivan, Ph.D.

HAY HOUSE, INC.
Carlsbad, California • New York City
London • Sydney • Johannesburg
Vancouver • Hong Kong • New Delhi

Published and distributed in the United States by: Hay House, Inc.:
www.hayhouse.com • *Published and distributed in Australia by:* Hay House
Australia Pty. Ltd.: www.hayhouse.com.au • *Published and distributed in the
United Kingdom by:* Hay House UK, Ltd.: www.hayhouse.co.uk • *Published and
distributed in the Republic of South Africa by:* Hay House SA (Pty), Ltd.:
www.hayhouse.co.za • *Distributed in Canada by:* Raincoast: www.raincoast.com
• *Published in India by:* Hay House Publishers India: www.hayhouse.co.in

Editorial supervision: Jill Kramer • *Design:* Riann Bender

Cover photos: Rock formations on a landscape, Olgas, Uluru-Kata Tjuta National
Park, Australia © Fred Kamphues/SuperStock; Silbury Hill, England © Steve
Alexander/www.temporarytemples.co.uk; Pyramid on a landscape, The Step
Pyramid of Zoser, Saqqara, Egypt © Yoshio Tomii/SuperStock.

Internal photos: p. 1, p. 45, p. 145, and p. 185 © age fotostock/SuperStock; p. 23
© Steve Vidler/SuperSTock; p. 67 © John Warden/SuperStock; p. 87 © Michele
Burgess/SuperStock; p. 111 © Fred Kamphues/SuperStock; p. 127 © Rona
Spencer; p. 153 © Angelo Cavalli/SuperStock; p. 165 © SuperStock,
Inc./SuperStock; p. 195 © Steve Alexander; p. 225 © Tony Currivan

Library of Congress Control Number: 2007921287

ISBN: 978-1-4019-1873-6

12 11 10 09   4 3 2 1
1st edition, January 2009

Printed in the United States of America

DEDICATION

I dedicate *The 13th Step*, with love, joy and gratitude, to:

My beloved mother, who has taught me that laughter is the greatest healer in the world;

my dear ex-husband Pete, who has shown me that an open heart is the path to freedom;

and

my darling husband and soul mate Tony, with whom I joyfully embrace all that love and life are and can be.

From the Editor: To our American readers, please note that for the most part, we have maintained the British style of spelling, grammar, punctuation, and syntax of the original text in order to preserve the editorial intent of the author, who hails from the United Kingdom.

CONTENTS

PREFACE

The 13th Step is the true story of ordinary people undertaking an extraordinary inner and outer journey. It shares the experiences of 13 sacred journeys around the world, which ultimately became an inner and outer odyssey of revelation of our human heritage and cosmic destiny.

The journeys were undertaken in the trust of higher guidance that I received from the Elohim, a group of etheric beings who have been the spiritual guardians of evolution within our Solar or 'Soular' System from its beginning.

The initial intention was clear: to activate the healing energies of 12 'Soular Discs', spiritual artifacts located at different sacred sites around the world. Gifted by the Elohim to the elders of Lemuria many millennia ago, they connect energetically with the collective psyche of humanity and the geomantic grid of the Earth. Activating their energies at this time would support individual and collective shifts of awareness.

The initial guidance was unequivocal: the 12 pilgrimages were to be completed by 'early November 2003' and, enigmatically, a '13th master key' was to be turned at Avebury on 23 December 2003. However, the higher purpose of the quest was only revealed as our experiences unfolded and our understanding deepened. Enabling profound healing and an awareness of our cosmic heritage and destiny, the journeys have brought forward a message of hope and reconciliation for the collective birthing of Heaven on Mother Earth. The 12 journeys culminated, as guided, on 23 December – the ancient 'day out of time' – with the enigma of the master key and the purpose of its turning being revealed and enacted.

And my work appeared to be complete.

But in 2006 the Elohim returned, guiding me to undertake a 13th journey…

The 13th Step is not only the true story of an inner and outer odyssey of revelation, but it offers each of us insights that reverberate with meaning and that we can incorporate to transform our own lives, to journey home to our inner wholeness and be in service to our collective ascension. As we continue on to 2012 and the birthing of a new age, its aim is to be an empowering and heart-centred way-shower to our personal and collective journey HoME – the birthing of Heaven on Mother Earth.

We are all fellow travellers on this path, and the native elders say that 'we are the ones we have been waiting for'. I am reminded of the following words, which were given to me in the midst of the Avebury landscape one beautiful morning:

> *In the commonality of our humanity, we are all ordinary*
> *In the commonality of our divinity, we are all*
> *extraordinary.*

And so we are.

Jude
Megiddo, Israel

ACKNOWLEDGEMENTS

To all my fellow travellers, thank you for enriching our journey with your love and for all that you have taught me:

Catherine Bennett, Renae Blanton, Janet Britton, Mavis Brown, Ann Buzenberg, August Cardinale, Helen Carr, Gillian Clarke-Hill, Hiroko Collins, Emma Comfort, Ramsey Coolidge, Tony Currivan, Betty Dahmer, Lynnclaire Dennis, Sylvia Drieser-Farnsworth, John Duncan, Doreen Duthie, Bill Eastman, Judith Eastman, Elizabeth Edenborough, Leilani Edwards, Magdalena Emerson, James Farnsworth, Annette Fernyhough, Ginny FitzRoy, Valerie Gambrill, Brian Gerhardt, Derriel Gilburn, Jennifer Grierson, Andrew Hahn, Terry Lynn Hartman, Cynthia Hodges, Pia Hoffman-Hansen, Flora Hoskin, Diahann Hughes, Richard Hutchens, Brian Jones, Erica Jones, Joanna Jones, Logan Jones, Liza Keast, Mary Kedl, Cynthia Kennard, Yvette Khoshab, Gabi Kikinger, Hannes Kikinger, Alan Knight, Helen Landis, Marilyn Lennon, Lara Leonard, Suzie Litton-Wood, Rosamaria Machado-Wilson, Carol McCutcheon, Joe McCutcheon, Jytte Brender McNair, Pete Arne McNair, Ian Martell, Tai Massari, Phil Medley, Sharon Mitchell, Deborah Molinari, Elizabeth Monson, Cynthia Mae Neill, Diana O'Shea, Dr Christine Page, Niki Patel, Ellis Pearce, Justina Pettifer, Nitya Richmond, Susan Roberts, Christine Rooney, Albert Rowe, Anita Runyan, Amanda Salmon, Yaeko Satomi, Anne Simpson, Kianna Smith, Rona Spencer, Catherine Stewart, Rebecca Street, Wendy Summerfield, Melinda Tiller, Marie Vertannes, Terry Ward, Sandra Wells, Mary White, Karin Wijeratne, Vivienne Wise, Lenia Zemenides and all those many others who accompanied us in Spirit.

To all those who made the journey possible, especially John Buzenberg and all the guides and teachers whose insights and wisdom enlightened our path.

To all of my Hay House family who support our collective journey of re-membering, especially Michelle Pilley, Jo Burgess and Jo Lal at Hay House UK. To my dear friend Jeannie Kar, without whose invaluable help the book would not have been shaped. And to my wonderful editor, Lizzie Hutchins.

To the Elohim, to Thoth and to all my discarnate friends, guides and guardians throughout all the cosmic realms, my deepest respect for your self-less service to humanity and Gaia and my wholehearted gratitude for all that you have taught and continue to teach me.

All I ask of you is forever to remember me as loving you.

☗ ☀ ☗

INTRODUCTION

As I levitated up and out of the deep water-filled shaft into the dazzlingly bright Egyptian sunlight, my mind raced back nine months to the day when my life had changed forever.

*****

For it was then, on 3 May 1998, enjoying the gentleness of a late spring afternoon in England, that I received the psychic guidance loud and very clear, the seemingly innocuous invitation: 'Come to Silbury Hill tomorrow.' The same age as the Great Pyramid at Giza, Silbury Hill is the greatest monumental mound in Europe. For many of those who are sensitive to Earth energies, it is also the energetic nexus of the sacred landscape around Avebury – the epicentre of the crop-circle phenomenon and my home for the last few years.

What a radiant morning! The bright blue sky was mirrored in the water laked around the hill. Approaching it with a quiet sense of anticipation, I saw a crop circle in the field of golden oilseed just to the south, which had literally appeared overnight.

As I gazed in appreciation, a psychic message, as loud and clear as the first, guided me not to enter the crop circle but to climb to the top of the hill.

On the summit I settled down to connect energetically with the hill and the full glory of the crop circle arrayed beneath me. This mysterious miracle created from a living and unharmed crop was nearly 200 feet across. Its pattern was that of a golden disc composed of an inner and outer circle, conjoined, I later discovered, by 33 curling 'flames'.

Attuning myself to Silbury Hill and the golden disc below, I was filled with a deep sense of peace, as though all my questions had been answered, but I didn't understand what those questions had been!

And without yet realizing it, I'd also energetically connected to an ancient golden disc etherically sited there, whose presence had been symbolically and energetically mirrored by the crop circle.

Back home in the throes of a busy day, my experience rapidly faded. Later that week, I was co-leading a workshop with Aluna Joy Yaxk'in, an American teacher of Mayan wisdom, who told us of a special place near Lake Titicaca in Peru. The image she showed was of a huge red rock with its vertical face sculpted with two upright channels and a human-sized 'door' carved into the centre.

As she described this as the portal of Amaru Muru, I felt a profound heart connection to the place. I had never seen it before in this life and Peru was a country I'd not visited. At that time I did not have the money to do so. Again, I was busy and the connection quickly became a memory.

*****

Two weeks later, I gave a short workshop in the Avebury landscape to an American group. Afterwards, their leader John Buzenberg, whom I'd only met for the first time that day, said that they'd enjoyed the session so much, would I teach with him in Peru?

It seemed I was destined to visit Peru. And though at that time I didn't know it, John also knew the portal of Amaru Muru well, and the man who had rediscovered it, Jorge Luis Delgado.

Another week passed and I received a call from someone who was leaving with another group to explore the Takla Makan region of far western China. He called to ask whether I could attune to my higher guidance for any insights concerning their journey. When I did so, I received three messages. The third of these was that he and his group would connect with a 'golden disc'. Again, at the time its significance didn't register on my conscious mind.

Calling to give him the messages, I discovered that the group had already departed. It was only on his return that he told me that my first two messages had been borne out and that the group had also connected with an etheric golden disc at a place called Rawak in the far west of China. His powerful experience of the disc was that it radiated the essence of unconditional love. Its energies had remained with him on his return home, aiding his work as a healer.

*****

Over the next few months, the mystery of the golden discs melted into the background as I struggled painfully with personal upheaval as my then husband fell in love with someone else.

Having always been the 'rescuer' and the one who coped throughout my life, I was terrified at the thought of feeling vulnerable, and staved off the inevitable as long as I could. One sunny day in the garden, my departing husband told me the truth – I had shut down my heart. As the truth and grief of that realization hit me, I suddenly saw how long ago I'd retreated from real feelings as a defence mechanism and how my perceived sanctuary had become a prison of my own making.

My heart broke open in that moment and I resolved that whatever the future held I would meet it with an open heart.

*****

Easier said than done, for by January of the following year I was at a very low ebb. In the aftermath of my marriage breakdown, despite all my efforts to hang on to my home and healing centre, financially I was on the brink of disaster.

Amidst the turmoil, I'd nonetheless co-organized a group journey to Egypt – a journey I now felt almost too depleted and energetically exhausted to undertake. But with the travel plans booked and paid for, I realized that the only sensible option was to proceed. And as I stood at this point of breakdown, I dimly sensed that somehow the Cosmos was offering me the possibility of a desperately needed breakthrough.

While we were based at Luxor, the great centre of temples and tombs, we had arranged to visit Abydos, whose mysterious temple, the Oseirion, is so ancient it has now sunk far below the level of the surrounding desert. That morning, the words 'Wear a swimsuit today' rushed urgently into my waking mind. Knowing that we were heading into the desert, I laughed at the apparent incongruity and dressed as usual.

Big mistake!

Arriving at Abydos, I felt a deep need to be alone. Appreciative of the group's understanding, I made my way to the threefold inner sanctum of the ancient gods Horus, Isis and Osiris, small chapels within the temple built by the pharaoh Seti I. There I asked for whatever inner-tuition or initiation I needed at that time.

As I entered the chapel dedicated to Osiris, a veil immediately seemed to shroud my eyes and I could feel the close presence of all three deities.

I then made my way through the temple and along the walled corridor covered in hieroglyphs leading to the Oseirion. Depicting the lineage of Osiris, Isis and Horus, the hieroglyphs speak of the ancient time when the deities themselves were deemed to rule Egypt. And as I passed by, I suddenly began to weep uncontrollably.

Emerging into the bright sunlight, misted through my tears, and still veiled, I slowly climbed down the steps of the Oseirion, vaguely noting that at this time of year the Nile waters shallowly covered its floor.

A powerful urge to walk into its inner sanctum then suddenly filled me. I took my shoes off, rolled up my jeans, took two steps and fell into a 35-foot shaft filled with water!

As the water closed over my head, I felt no panic and knew that this was my initiation.

*****

The very next moment I was sitting back on the steps, soaking wet, with no recollection of how I had emerged from the deep vertical-sided shaft.

The veil of Isis was now drawn back and my vision felt clearer than ever before. And between laughing and crying, I appreciated how my early-morning voice had tried to save me from several hours of wet underwear.

Only later was I able to realize that I had literally levitated from that water-filled chamber of initiation.

Over the next three days, I was also shocked to find that my kundalini energy had been spontaneously raised and now flowed freely throughout my body. This energy lies coiled within each of us at the base of our spine until we spiritually awaken. When raised, its flow enables us to progressively access higher levels of awareness.

Some time afterwards, I also discovered that the ancient temple initiation of Osiris had been by baptism in water. Thank you, Osiris, Isis and Horus.

Arriving back from Egypt energetically and physically transformed but exhausted, I spent the next three weeks confined to bed. The moment I recovered, with the sense of liberation that had been birthed at Abydos, I happily arranged to sell my house and go with the flow of the Cosmos into an unknown future.

*****

I moved into a tiny rented cottage, standing alone in a quiet valley, just in time for the lunar and solar eclipses of 28 July, and

11 August 1999, whose energies powerfully ushered in this new beginning for me. And by October, I was ready to travel to Peru to journey with John, wisdom teacher Bonita Luz and a group of fellow travellers.

Our journey in Peru was magical. Immersing myself in the essence of Mother Earth, known to the Peruvian people as Pacha Mama, and exploring places such as Ollantaytambo and Machu Picchu was a tonic for my soul.

When we arrived at Lake Titicaca we met Jorge Delgado, who shared with us the legend of the portal of Amaru Muru. He told us of the mythic Lord Amaru and his companion, Lady Amara, elders of the ancient Pacific Empire of Lemuria, who had taken a 'Solar' or 'Soular Disc' to Lake Titicaca.

Describing the physical form of the multi-dimensional artifact as being a golden disc, Jorge went on to share how, at the time of the Incas (the children of the Sun), the priceless Disc had been taken to Cusco, the physical and energetic centre of the Incan Empire. There, in the Corocancha, the House of the Sun, it had remained until the priests had spirited it back to Lake Titicaca before the fall of the Incan Empire to the Spanish conquistadors.

The next day, when Jorge guided us to the portal, I again felt the deep connection I had first experienced a year before and half a world away in Avebury and sensed the stirrings of a memory from an ancient past. And yet something was holding me back from passing through the portal. That was to take a much longer inner and outer quest and nearly three more years.

The surface of Lake Titicaca is strewn with a number of float-ing islands constructed of reeds, on which the villagers of the lake make their home. Our final destination was such an island, gently rising and falling in the embrace of the water. Here Bonita led the group in a meditation to energetically connect with the Lemurian Soular Disc.

As I opened myself to its energies, an all-embracing feeling of unconditional love overwhelmed me. For the first time in my life

I felt truly home. My heart burst and I wept with a remembering beyond joy and sorrow.

There was no going back.

*****

Back in England, I nestled in the sanctuary of my tiny cottage and allowed a torrent of understanding and higher guidance to flood through me. For the next six months, the daily wonders of my inner life were held safe and gently grounded by the quiet of my outer existence.

By March of the new millennium, the warp and weft of an incredible tapestry of understanding had begun to be woven. Inwardly I knew that we had indeed connected with the energies of an ancient Lemurian Soular Disc at Lake Titicaca. But as my awareness continued to unfold, I discovered that this Peruvian Disc was one of 12 positioned around the Earth.

The powerful clairaudient guidance of my childhood returned and clearly revealed the Discs as multi-dimensional 'moderators, modulators and facilitators of consciousness'. They connect with the etheric planetary grid, which is in the geometric form of a dodecahedron, each of its 12 pentagonal faces being anchored energetically by one of the Discs.

As each is activated, I was guided that they will facilitate our collective awakening from our spiritual amnesia and the illusion of separation. They are helping us re-member who we really are and our highest spiritual connection with the Cosmos.

While hitherto I'd felt that my guidance concerning the Soular Discs was emanating from a group of beings of the greatest integrity, until now I had been unaware of exactly who they were. Now, asking me to refer to them collectively as the Elohim, they explained that since its inception they have been the aetheric guardians of our Solar (or 'Soular') System and its evolution. They reveal their presence and guidance only rarely. They are doing so now, they say, because a great evolutionary shift is imminent, not only for humanity, but for the Earth and our entire Soular System.

In a flash of insight I could also now see that my overwhelming experience of the Soular Disc at Lake Titicaca had also integrated my initial and fleeting connections with three of the other Discs – those present at Silbury Hill, Rawak in western China and the Oseirion in Egypt.

While the guidance of the Elohim showed me that the remaining eight Discs were energetically centred in South Africa, Alaska, Australia, New Zealand, Easter Island, Antarctica, Hawaii and the Indian Ocean, details of their exact locations were only to emerge over time. Connecting with each one of them was clearly meant to be a co-creative and unfolding effort and would, it turned out, involve many others in a collective journey of discovery and transformation.

*****

Much more understanding was to await its perfect time to emerge, but my immediate guidance was clear and unequivocal – I was to offer group journeys to activate the healing energies of each of the Discs.

The Elohim also gave us a very specific time-frame in which to complete these 12 pilgrimages – 'by early November 2003'. And for good measure, I was told that we should 'turn the 13th master key at Avebury on 23 December 2003'.

Despite my asking, the Elohim offered no understanding of why these timings were important, what the 13th master key was or why it needed to be turned at Avebury. We were to complete the first three journeys before that awareness would begin to be revealed. And only at the completion of the 12th journey were we to unveil the mystery of the 13th 'master key'.

Not really knowing how to take the first step, I called John who, without hesitation, gave his loving support to arranging the journeys. All he needed from me was direction on the sequence, dates and itinerary.

My higher guidance was to connect with three Discs during 2001, four during 2002 and the remaining five in 2003, culminating in early November 2003 at the Disc where it all began – Silbury Hill. And finally we were to turn the enigmatic 'master key' on 23 December of that year – whatever that meant.

Attuning again, I knew – again without understanding why – that the first three journeys during 2001 were to be to Egypt, Africa and China.

It appeared that while the Elohim would guide my path, they would do so only to the extent we needed to be able to take the next step. This would be an ongoing lesson in trust and, as we would discover again and again, it encouraged and indeed required us to live in the present moment.

I was also told that if I could see the magnitude of the entire quest, I wouldn't be able to begin it. In hindsight, I thank the Elohim for their compassion and wisdom. For if I had understood at the beginning what would unfold, I'm not sure I would have had the courage to take the first step.

So, as I prepared to return to Egypt to activate the 1st Soular Disc, I took a very deep breath and a leap of faith.

卍 卍 卍

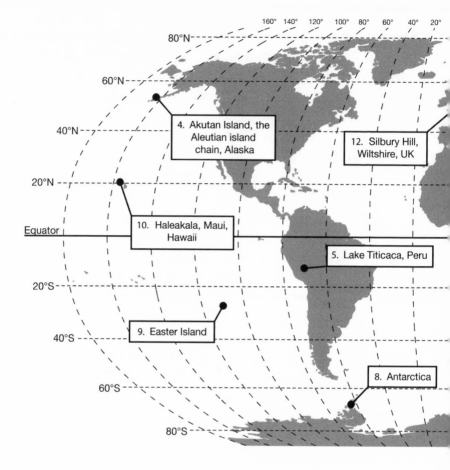

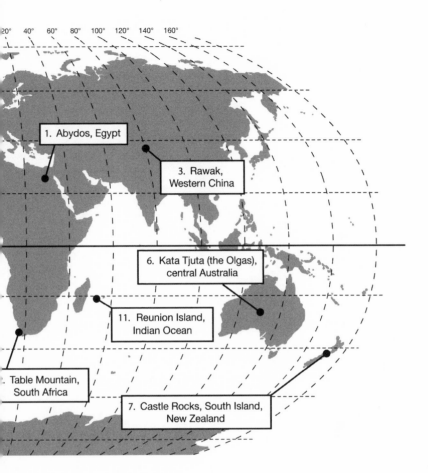

20° 40° 60° 80° 100° 120° 140° 160°

1. Abydos, Egypt

3. Rawak, Western China

6. Kata Tjuta (the Olgas), central Australia

11. Reunion Island, Indian Ocean

. Table Mountain, South Africa

7. Castle Rocks, South Island, New Zealand

CHAPTER 1

Egypt

CHAPTER 1

EGYPT

February 2001

Multi-dimensional portals are now opening within the ancient sacred places of the Earth, anchoring higher vibrational energies to help us awaken from our spiritual amnesia. In Egypt, these inner sanctums have been safeguarded by the archetypal beings we know as their gods and goddesses, held in trust until this time of re-membering.

It was the perfect journey to commence our three-year odyssey. We planned to follow the flow of the life-giving Nile river from Abu Simbel in the far south to the pyramids of Giza in the north. And midway between the two, at the Oseirion at Abydos, we hoped to activate the energies of the Soular Disc.

Our inner journey of discovery also began to unfold as we each connected with eight deities whose presence pervades the land that Thoth, the Egyptian god of wisdom, terms the 'temple of the Cosmos'. Representing two cosmic trinities, one of light – Osiris, Isis and Horus – and one of shadow – Set, Nephthys and Anubis – each combines the cosmic essence of male, female and child energies.

As we would experience, each also embodies certain attributes: Osiris, initiatory power; Isis, nurturing love; Horus, far-sighted vision; Set, transformational courage; Nephthys, the clarity of inner reflection; and Anubis, exploratory openness. In addition, the partnership of Hathor–Sekhmet offers us spiritual abundance and strength of purpose, and Maat offers the energies of harmonious balance.

Each traveller was invited to explore their own inner connection with these archetypal beings, and I also felt our entire journey being gently guided by Thoth himself.

*****

The bright morning Sun blazed in a clear azure sky as I walked lazily from our hotel at Abu Simbel towards the paired temples of the pharaoh Rameses II and his beloved wife Nefetari.

Originally, the two temples were carved into the rock of the cliff excavated by the immense flow of the Nile floods. When the Aswan High Dam was built in the 1960s, the dammed waters would have drowned the temples had they not been moved, stone by stone, to safer ground. Now they stand beyond the thin ribbon of rich river-fed land with their backs to the desert that stretches into the vast distance.

Over three millennia ago, Rameses II ruled Egypt for nearly seven decades and was one of the most powerful pharaohs in its long history. Huge statues of him seated at the entrance to his temple at Abu Simbel dwarf visitors.

Rameses's manifest power is very strong here and in the dark recesses of his temple I could feel the grounding of my own intention and the courage to be true to the odyssey of the next three years.

In contrast, the temple of Nefetari, dedicated to Hathor, felt gentle and joyous, and as the day wore on I could see that the group, benignly held in her nurturing embrace, was rapidly bonding. It felt like the reunion of family rather than, for many, a first meeting of strangers.

*****

Boarding the cruise boat that was to be our home for the following few days, we began the journey north towards Luxor, flowing at the slow pace of the river.

On our way, we moored at the village of Edfu to experience its great temple dedicated to the falcon-headed Horus. Every pharaoh of Egypt was perceived as the embodiment of Horus, whose far-sightedness and strength manifested and maintained the cosmic order of the land. And as we entered the portal to the temple's sacred precincts, we were flanked by the potent presence of two huge falcons carved from granite.

From the mythological beginnings of ancient Egypt, the complementary nature of light and dark was enshrined in legend and both were perceived as necessary to the ultimate balance of the Cosmos. Within the temple, the interplay of bright sunlight alternating with deep shadow revealed, along the walls of the western corridor, a carved relief of this metaphysical insight in the form of the eternal battle between Horus and Set – the forces of order and chaos.

As we were guided around the inner sanctums of the temple, which would once have only been trod by initiates, I felt this cosmic interplay resonate within me and realized that during our journey we would need to connect with and embrace both the light and shadow within ourselves before we could heal.

Suddenly, I knew at a deep level what healing really meant. For in that moment I understood that when our partial perception of light and shadow becomes balanced and integrated within ourselves, we are able to transcend our sense of separation and re-member the wholeness of who we really are.

*****

Comfortable on our floating home, we continued to deepen our friendships and all were supportive when we suggested a group healing process facilitated by two of our number, Andrew and Ramsey, both of whom were therapists. While it was made clear that anyone could opt out of the process at any time, nearly every-one chose to stay.

The healing process was based on group attunement, with intuitive and dowsed responses to questions and insights as they arose. Our initial intention was to gain a deeper sense of why each of us, and the group as a whole, had chosen to join this journey. Our second was to reveal whether, as individuals or collectively, there were any attitudes or behaviour that might be blockages to our inner journey of discovery. We would then seek to understand what was happening, what to do to resolve and release any issues, and what lessons we could learn from our experience.

As we began, almost immediately a story began to emerge of an earlier life that it appeared many of us had shared. This is our story:

At some time during the long millennia of the great civilization that was ancient Egypt, a boy and girl grew up together. The bonds that connected them were deep and loving, but as they became adults their paths diverged. The boy grew to be a powerful priest of Set, while the girl was chosen to be a priestess of Hathor. The man followed a dark and lonely road and in his quest for power delved ever more deeply into the occult arts. The girl, however, chose the road of light and was ultimately initiated as a member of a brotherhood of light.

The brotherhood became aware of the growing danger of the dark priest of Set and, in their fear and judgement, sought to destroy him. Knowing how powerful he had become, they realized that the only way of overcoming him was by deceit.

There was only one person the deeply suspicious dark priest trusted – his childhood friend, who loved him as he loved her. The priestess of light fought against this perceived need for betrayal, but finally, convinced that it was the only way to defeat her friend, lured him into the trap set by the brotherhood of light.

It resulted in his terrible death. And to ensure that his powerful spirit had no way of returning, she then cut out his heart – and in doing so, condemned her own to die within her.

In their continuing fear of the influence of the dark priest, the brotherhood of light then mercilessly condemned to death all those associated with him.

Overwhelmed by the grief of her betrayal, the priestess of light could do nothing to save them.

As we explored our group experience of this past-life memory, many of us realized that we each had played a role in the story. As we came to terms with our understanding, we also began to appreciate the gift of the archetypal healing being offered to us.

Even those with no conscious recollection of that time, or who perceived it as a metaphor, gained a profound realization: that when we judge or are unwilling to embrace our own inner shadow, its energies and emotions become more isolated and powerful.

The actions of the brotherhood of light also showed us, in an unavoidably painful way, how light by itself is as unbalanced as shadow, and only by embracing all that we are can we hope to heal.

As we continued our group process of re-membering, we came to appreciate that it was not so much the actions themselves but the intention behind them that had resulted in the unbalanced duality continuing to play out. For had the brotherhood of light acted from love rather than fear, their compassionate yet empowered actions against the dark priest would have brought healing to both.

My own experience in the revelation of this past-life story was deeply challenging, as it was I who had been the priestess of light, and my grief felt very real and very present. Especially painful was that the energies of the dark priest were embodied within the group in my friend Brian. But, as we lovingly acknowledged the trauma of that previous life together, we knew that our healing had begun and would now continue to its completion.

*****

Still in the throes of dealing with these revelations, we arrived at Luxor and set off to explore the vast temple complex of Karnak.

Here, quietly hidden away, is, for me, one of the most powerful places in the whole of Egypt. The chapel of the lioness-headed Sekhmet is a tiny room in the sanctuary dedicated to her consort Ptah, who was to the ancient Egyptians the archetype of form and the shaping force of the Cosmos.

Here stands a basalt statue of Sekhmet that has remained in this place through the ebb and flow of history for over three millennia. A small window high in the chapel allows light to gently bathe her, and for me and many others, this first sight of her is overwhelming.

As we entered her presence we felt the fire of her creative power – the lioness, fierce in anger and infinitely gentle in love. Over many years Sekhmet, partnered with Hathor, has provided me with the spiritual empowerment and abundance to see through major challenges. I welcomed her strength now as we sought to heal the past.

Silently standing together, each of us in our own way asked for her guidance to resolve and release whatever trauma we needed to, and to help us embody the realization that unifies light and shadow.

On leaving, I offered a prayer of gratitude to her and prepared to journey on.

*****

From the earliest pre-dynastic records of ancient Egypt, Abydos has been the sacred centre of the veneration of Osiris, the lord of the netherworld. In my early childhood I'd read the myth of Osiris. This tells how he bestowed the gift of civilization on Egypt and how, as he journeyed far and wide, sharing his benevolent wisdom, his consort Isis remained to steward the land on his behalf.

Osiris's brother Set, desiring Isis and jealous of his sibling, plotted to kill him. Deceiving Osiris into lying in a specially constructed coffin, he and his fellow plotters then sealed it and threw it into the Nile, intending Osiris to be lost forever.

Isis was bereft at the loss of her husband. And after many adventures and with the help of her sister Nephthys, Set's consort, and the wise and resourceful Thoth, she discovered his body.

Through her deep love, she was then able to be magically impregnated by Osiris with their son Horus, who, by ultimately overcoming Set, remanifested cosmic order. His archetypal power and far-sightedness were then embodied in the pharaohs of the many dynasties that for many thousands of years afterwards ruled the land of Egypt.

The saga of Osiris embodies the ultimate essence of the cosmic cycles of birth, life, death and rebirth. And every year for many millennia until the recent creation of the Aswan High Dam, the three seasons of Egypt, denoted by the Nile flood, its subsidence and subsequent drought, continued to replay the story of his life, death and resurrection.

As such Osiris was also seen to embody the essence of spiritual initiation, which in Egypt, as in many other traditions, is perceived as being comprised of three parts. The first is the initiate's instigation of the circumstances that offer the opportunity for such an inner journey of discovery. The ultimate purpose of spiritual initiation is to gain a more profound inner awareness of the Cosmos and our place within it. This 'inner-tuition' gained by the initiatory experience forms the second part of the process. The third part is the integration of the experience, physically, emotionally, mentally and, most importantly, within the psyche of the initiate.

Each of us had already undergone the first part of the initiation of this journey by our willingness to participate. Our inner-intuition would now continue as we journeyed on to Abydos.

*****

Abydos is the location of the ancient Oseirion, the tomb of Osiris and my place of initiatory baptism two years before. From my experience then and my guidance since, I also now knew that this was the epicentre of the energies of one of the 12 Soular Discs located around the Earth.

But, as I had done then, we first visited the later temple built by the pharaoh Seti I to seek within its inner shrines the blessings of Osiris, Isis and Horus.

Once again I walked down the ramp towards the Oseirion, this time with my travelling companions, and we were saddened to notice how poorly it was stewarded, the authorities apparently unaware of its significance.

The water at the floor level of the Oseirion was lower than I had experienced in the past. Twice before I'd attempted to walk into its dome-roofed inner chamber. The first time, I had undergone my transformational rite of baptism. The second, on a private visit one year before, I'd placed my foot into another pool of water at the very threshold of the inner chamber. While it was shallow, I was alerted that I was not meant to go any farther at that time.

Now, here with the intention to activate the Soular Disc, I was unsure whether I would personally be invited into the chamber.

Following the others who were passing without pause over the threshold, I waited, uncertain until I felt a gentle sense of welcome greet me.

Inside the large echoing chamber we could hear the bats wheeling high up in the vaulted roof. We each meditated and opened ourselves to the universal heart energy of the Soular Disc that powerfully surrounded and embraced us.

For many of us, our awareness of unity consciousness, beyond and underlying the creative dance of light and shadow, was joyously birthed in that moment. Heartbreakingly beautiful visions came to me of swirling energies of multi-hued light spiralling around and through me. And I felt deep with myself a sense of cosmic benevolence – golden, peaceful and unconditionally loving.

For some of us, the glimpse of a love so all-embracing was overwhelming and our tears freely flowed. Those who felt its gentle blessing were changed forever and tentatively we began to understand the possibility of its embodiment within us.

Later, sharing our experiences, everyone laughed as one of us, recollecting the sad shabbiness of the surroundings of the Oseirion, told of her earlier vision of an incredibly bright light coming out of a garbage can!

In our euphoria, we didn't realize that although we had connected powerfully with the Disc, its culminating activation was still to come in an unexpected and yet perfect way at the very end of our journey.

*****

Before we travelled on to Cairo, John needed to leave us and return to the USA. I was now waking in the early hours of each morning with an ever-deepening understanding of the Soular Discs and how they supported our personal and collective healing through direct experience and insights. Each day I facilitated our energetic work and, in John's absence, dealt with the practicalities of our journey.

Unable to eat much, I began to lose weight at a rate that, had I considered it, would have been alarming. I was becoming lighter and emptier each day, as though I was somehow preparing myself for what was still to come.

*****

Back in Cairo, we explored the Egyptian Museum, a vast treasure trove of the glories of ancient Egypt. It included the amazingly rich discoveries from the tomb of the boy king Tutankhamun, who ruled for a brief time at the turbulent end of the Eighteenth Dynasty, and also housed statues of the pharaoh Akhenaten, claimed by some Egyptologists to be Tutankhamun's father.

Akhenaten's rule was revolutionary. He overturned established priesthoods throughout Egypt and, from his new capital at Amarna, dictated that only worship of the disc of the Sun – the Aten – was allowed.

For some time I'd had a sense that Akhenaten's connection with the Aten resonated in some way with my unfolding understanding of the Soular Discs. As we were guided around the museum, I took the opportunity to spend some time in a room replete with statues of him. Jostled by other visitors and their ever-present bustle, I still found that the power of the statues overcame all distractions and I was able to attune to Akhenaten's imprinted energy.

My inner vision revealed a time when the long reign of Akhenaten's father, Amenhotep III, was drawing to a close. The powerful priesthoods, seeing the end of an era, were conspiring, for in Akhenaten they saw the dangerous beginnings of heresy and a reduction of their own influence and prosperity.

Akhenaten was a high-level initiate. I sensed his foreboding that after a lengthy time of stability in Egypt there was to come a period of great turbulence, which the corrupt priesthoods would be unable to prevent. As pharaoh, and thus the metaphysical embodiment of Horus, he perceived that his divine role was to maintain the sacred order. And in returning to the Sun, the greatest metaphysical and physical symbol of unity in the Egyptian world, he allied himself to its power.

By locating his newly built capital city of Amarna at the exact geographical centre of Egypt and aligning its grid layout to the eastern horizon and the rising Sun, Akhenaten further augmented the visible power of the Aten and its ability to maintain the balance and stability of the land.

In that small room in the museum, I realized too that Akhenaten had been aware of the Soular Disc at Abydos. Surrounded by the comings and goings of other visitors, I felt his gentle yet powerful presence and understood that he had recognized and connected to the Disc's energy.

I could now sense that Akhenaten had sought to reconnect with unity and thus to sustain the idealized order of the Cosmos. Yet while the unity that underlies its diversity is eternal, the dance of creation goes on. The energies through which consciousness is expressed are ever-changing and, whether within an individual human life or through the rise and fall of civilizations, the waves of birth, life, death and rebirth must all ebb and flow in their perfect season.

So it was for Egypt. Despite his efforts, Akhenaten's reign only lasted for 17 years and its end was shrouded in mystery. His monotheistic teachings, however, lived on in the revelations of Moses and the emergent beliefs of the Hebrews. And so regardless of the priests and future pharaohs who attempted to excise Akhenaten from history, his philosophy persisted and ultimately became the genesis of the three world religions of Judaism, Christianity and Islam.

As I felt the ripple of Akhenaten's presence fade, I knew that we still had work to do together and a small seed was planted within my psyche, there to lie dormant for the time being. I knew that at the right time its purpose would germinate in service to healing the schisms of religious divergence and the mayhem it would unleash.

*****

Nothing prepares you for your first sight of the three huge pyramids of Khufu, Khafre and Menkaure. Their iconic presence bestrides the plateau of Giza.

Khufu's pyramid, the largest, is rightly called the Great Pyramid and is the only one of the seven wonders of the ancient world to survive to the present day. Positioned with miraculous accuracy to the cardinal points of north, south, east and west, it marks the centre of the landmasses of the Earth. Together, located next to the earthly Nile that reflects the heavenly river of the Milky Way, the three pyramids appear to reflect the three stars of Orion's Belt, cosmologically connecting Heaven and Earth.

A tiny figure standing at the base of the Great Pyramid, I remembered the events of two years before.

Then, as I had woken from a vivid dream just before leaving home for Egypt, where I was destined to undergo my initiation at Abydos and there connect unconsciously with the Soular Disc, an image and the words 'This is the symbol of Enki' had echoed in my mind.

The symbol of my dream had clearly depicted three vertically converging lines, the left and right being red and white respectively and the centre line black. At their upper points they had been met by a black horizontal line and above this had emerged the rays of a radiant light.

At the time, the only 'Enki' of whom I was aware was an ancient Sumerian god, one of the legendary Annunaki, extraterrestrial beings originating from the reputed '12th' planet of our Soular System.

During that journey, I'd shared my dream with the group I was co-leading and described the symbol of Enki. As we had travelled through Egypt, we had gradually come to understand that the symbol represented the coming together and balancing of the energies of the three cosmic principles of 'male', 'female' and 'child' and they were somehow, through darkness, to activate a form of light. How this connected with Enki, however, neither I nor any of my companions had any idea.

From a lifetime of fascinated study of ancient Egypt I'd perceived that the three vast pyramids at Giza embodied this cosmic trinity: the Great Pyramid of Khufu the 'male' principle, Khafre's pyramid the 'female' and the smallest of the three, Menkaure's pyramid, the 'child'. Now, as our group meditated together, we intuitively felt that the red line of the symbol equated to Khufu's pyramid, as its internal so-called King's Chamber was constructed of red granite, and that the white line symbolized Khafre's pyramid, whose only inner chamber was constructed of white limestone. The black central line, then, seemed to us to represent Menkaure's pyramid.

The greater understanding of my dream was about to be revealed to us in an amazing way.

Our itinerary brought us to Giza at the end of our journey and during our private access in the Great Pyramid of Khufu we followed our evolving guidance and connected energetically with the 'male' aspect of the cosmic trinity embodied there.

The next day we'd planned to connect with the cosmic 'female' energies at Khafre's pyramid and then to bring the male and female energies together at the pyramid of Menkaure, the embodiment of the cosmic child.

That morning we walked from our hotel onto the plateau, not realizing that overnight the mullahs had consulted the phase of the Moon and declared the end of the month-long observance of Ramadan – the Islamic holy period of fasting. The scene that met us was unbelievable. In celebration of the festival that marked the end of Ramadan, the entire population of Cairo appeared to be there – men, women and children – with the black robes of the women predominating and transforming the plateau into a dark seething mass of people.

Virtually no other tourists were present and as we slowly made our way through the crowd to Khafre's pyramid, I realized that we were encountering the symbolic darkness of my dream.

At the quietest of times it's difficult to find a few moments of peace around and within the pyramids, but now it seemed it would be impossible. Yet the impossible happened.

As we climbed the ascending passage into Khafre's inner chamber, no other visitors sought to enter. And, easily and without any sense of hurrying, we were able to carry out our purpose of attuning to the cosmic female energies there.

Re-emerging into the hubbub of the crowd, we then walked in silence to the pyramid of Menkaure, where the energies of the cosmic child are embodied. At the base of the vast bulk of the pyramid are the ruins of the small temple where we'd been guided to manifest my dream message. Here we were to bring the trinity of energies together and, through the dark, to activate the light.

We intuitively positioned ourselves to begin the work, but the local children, intrigued by our presence, would not quiet. Suddenly an ancient guard materialized out of the shadows and with a single word silenced the kids, who settled down to take their apparently predestined places around us.

As we attuned to our purpose, I felt an incredible power suddenly surge through me and up through the pyramid. Looking up, I saw with both my inner and outer vision an intense column of golden light emerge from its summit. Shooting up into the sky, it appeared to explode into a beautiful starburst, forming a golden net of light stretching beyond the horizon.

Later, as we shared our experiences, it emerged that three of us had vividly experienced this same vision. We three would also experience the same aftermath when on our return home we were all utterly drained of energy for several weeks.

Months later, on hearing our story, a friend suggested that I read *The Mars Mystery* by Graham Hancock, Robert Bauval and John Grigsby. The book describes the cataclysmic history of the Earth and how scientists are progressively appreciating how global catastrophes have resulted from the impact or near misses of interplanetary bodies such as comets that roam our Soular System.

I read with growing interest that governments had recently begun to invest in and co-ordinate efforts to detect such risks. The NASA website dedicated to this work is named after a comet that lies within a vast ring of such debris. The Earth passes through this ring twice yearly. And each June and November we experience our transit in the form of meteor showers, named Taurids after the constellation of Taurus from which they appear to emanate.

Much of this cometary minefield is comprised of tiny chunks of rock. But within its depths there are huge mountain-sized behemoths and at least one that may be larger than that likely to have caused the annihilation of the dinosaurs 65 million years ago. In amazement, I saw that the comet's name was Encke.

Suddenly remembering our vision of the vast golden web of light, I wondered. Had our work been to reactivate an energetic net of protection for the Earth?

In my heart, I felt that it had.

Months later still, as I looked up a reference in a book on the crop circle phenomenon, I happened to skip a few pages, and there was the symbol that I had seen in my dream. The caption, which related to Sumerian myths, stated, 'This is the symbol of the *Nin Gur*, the leader of whom was Enki'!

*****

Now, returning once more to Giza, I had a deep feeling that our activation of the Soular Disc at Abydos was incomplete without connecting somehow with the cosmic trinity embodied in the three pyramids.

I was unsure how we should do this, but I shouldn't have worried. For it appeared that the Elohim were ensuring that the process was already being set in place. Some days before, as we were cruising from Abu Simbel to Luxor, three of the group had, unbeknownst to me, approached John to see whether they could climb Menkaure's pyramid. Independently, I'd already arranged to stay on in Egypt after the group left. Also feeling a deep need to climb that pyramid, I'd planned to do so unobtrusively then. It was only when I mentioned this that I became aware of the others' plan and we realized that a single climb was the best option. At the time, our group process was continuing and I felt it was appropriate to suggest to Brian that he too join the ascent of the pyramid.

The proposal had been initiated independently. Also, given its physical and logistical difficulties – not least because such climbs are prohibited by the Egyptian authorities, who are rightly nervous of accidents – neither John nor I had, at that time, felt it needful to share it with the group. However, we had travelled an amazing outer journey together and we'd also shared a profound inner journey to heal and integrate the separation of our shadow. At its heart was an understanding that inclusion, not exclusion, is the only way to wholeness. Now, only a couple of days before the climb, I realized we must share knowledge of it with the others, even while recognizing how they might react to the unexpected news and the realization that no more than the five of us could actually make the ascent.

To my relief, they were magnificent. While being lovingly true in speaking of their disappointment and hurt at not being initially consulted, everyone generously accepted my apology and whole-heartedly supported the climb, which we now truly felt was on behalf of us all.

On the evening of the ascent, which would take place overnight, the five of us met to share a meal. Despite the wonderful restaurant service we'd received until then, our order did not appear. After a while, its continuing non-appearance inexorably reduced our time to eat. Eventually, as we were reluctantly preparing to leave, the food arrived! We didn't have time to eat it there, so the hotel staff kindly wrapped it and we took it with us.

We soon arrived at the home of the aged but incredibly agile gentleman who was to be our guide during the climb. By now we had begun to sense that our energetic work required us not to eat beforehand and we were pleased to offer our long-awaited meal to his family to enjoy.

Hours slipped by. Near midnight the signal came that it was time to leave and we stepped outside into the warm night to the sight of five patient camels, our ships of the desert, waiting for us to voyage into the dark.

The five of us, with our guide leading the way, rode into the desert night.

*****

Looking up, the only stars I could see in the cloudy night sky, perhaps inevitably, were the three stars forming the belt of Orion, visibly connecting the energies of the three pyramids to their cosmic counterparts.

Feeling the energy of the dark priest now ominously swirling around Brian, I knew that for our work to be complete and the Abydos Soular Disc fully activated, the light and the shadow needed to be reconciled. Somehow we would need the re-soulution of the cosmic trinity of light embodied by Osiris, Isis and Horus with that of the shadow embodied by Set, Nephthys and Anubis.

As we began to climb the vast bulk of the pyramid, the night around us was still, as though holding its breath. A mist seemed to envelop us as our world diminished to a focus on each uneven and waist-high step of the pyramid. After what seemed an age, our guide brought us safely to cluster below the small summit and our three companions went first to the high place.

When it was the turn of Brian and me, I could feel the love of the entire group supporting us. It suddenly felt very simple to open our hearts, release all judgement or expectation and envisage bringing the two trinities of energy together. After all the fear and uncertainty, it felt the easiest thing in the world. And as the cosmic trinities reconciled within us, the unconditionally loving embrace of their communion overwhelmed me.

Immediately, both Brian and I saw in our inner vision the brightness of the activated energies of the Soular Disc at Abydos and knew that our work there was finally complete.

*****

Back home, I had time to reflect on our journey and began to gain deeper understanding.

Initially, I'd perceived the purpose of the journeys as solely to activate the 12 Soular Discs. Yet in Egypt it had become clear that our experiences and the understanding and healing which arose throughout the journey itself were crucial to the awareness and intention we would then bring to the actual activation of each Disc. And, like pilgrims before us throughout the ages, we had begun to discover that the journey *is* the destination.

The activation of the Disc had activated something in me too. In the weeks following the journey I was intimately aware that a new energy centre that transcended my sense of self was beginning to open.

The universal heart of this 8th chakra remained open like a blossom in the warmth of a cosmic Sun. I pondered on its energies and those of other transpersonal chakras that I was becoming aware were now becoming accessible, not only to me and my fellow travellers, but to ever more people around the planet. Step by step, we were to become conscious of our expanded 12-fold chakra system, which profoundly resonates with the consciousness of the living Earth and our entire Soular System as a 13th collective soul.

Now, as we continued to connect energetically with these higher vibrations that expanded our energy field beyond our human personality, we were gaining glimpses of the progressive re-membering of our soular memory. We were discovering that the 8th chakra, of the universal heart, which most people were feeling as an energy centre positioned between their personal heart and throat chakras, is the portal to these higher connections.

I was also being guided to combine the energies of three of our personal chakras – those of the heart, alter major and solar plexus – and raise their vibrations to that of the 8th chakra.

The alter-major chakra, at the base of our skull, is sometimes called the breath of God. And this epicentre of the energies of our higher mind is now opening and connecting with the 6th and 7th chakras of the third eye and crown.

The trinity essence of the 8th chakra thus creates a portal to transcend the personal heart, mind and will. Unconditional love is the essence of this connection and I was beginning to experience directly how the opening of this energy centre is a joyous portal of awareness to an understanding of the higher consciousness that guides our human experience.

Integrating the cosmic trinities of light and shadow on the summit of Menkaure's pyramid had been the cosmic key to the opening of the universal heart within us.

*****

The Elohim had guided me that the second journey, to South Africa, should take place in June, four months after my return from Egypt.

Several days after receiving this specific date, I discovered that there was to be a total eclipse of the Sun on the solstice of 21 June and that its line of totality would arc over Africa. And I marvelled once again at how the synchronicities of the journeys were unfolding.

My guidance had also recently revealed that the energies of the Disc in South Africa were centred at the great monolith of Table Mountain at the southern tip of the continent. But as yet I had no intimation of the exact location.

And as I left for Africa, while trusting that somehow it would find us, I wondered what further revelations awaited us.

☒ ☒ ☒

CHAPTER 2

Africa

CHAPTER 2

AFRICA

June 2001

The Great Rift Valley of Africa is a vast geological rupture that extends the entire length of the continent. As part of my work as a cosmic geomancer facilitating healing and wholeness, I'd been attuning to its energies for some time. And I'd gained the understanding that it held the schisms of the 'rifted' energetic history of our human lineage.

The earliest human remains have been discovered in Olduvai Gorge in the heart of the Rift. The spiritual seed-point at the time of the pharaoh Akhenaten in Egypt had led to Judaism, Christianity and Islam and their subsequent religious rifts. Rwanda, geographically at the centre of the Rift, had for the past 10 years been enmeshed in tribal genocide and, through the use of rape as a weapon of war by HIV-positive soldiers, been an embodiment of the rift between male and female. And Zimbabwe, on the intersection of the path of totality of this coming eclipse and the Rift, was continuing to express deep racial tensions between black and white.

It was only after receiving guidance that the 2nd Soular Disc was at Table Mountain at the southern tip of Africa that I realized that it effectively held the southern 'pole' of these Rift energies and understood that the Disc at Abydos in Egypt held the northern 'pole'. Activating both, supported by the cosmic energies of the solar eclipse, would, we hoped, open the doorway of an opportunity to begin to release the energetic imprint of our rifted heritage.

*****

A total eclipse of the Sun is an awesome experience. The energies present in this cosmic balancing of light and shadow, the journey through the darkness and the re-emergence of the light, resonate with and embody our own inner spiritual journey and its outer physical reflection. That such an event was to take place at the solstice, when the combined energies of Sun, Moon and Earth were at their peak, felt very synchronous and auspicious. This momentous event would create a path of totality – the arced track over which the disc of the Moon completely covers that of the Sun – from the southern Atlantic Ocean, through central Africa and over the Rift, continuing until its completion in the southern Indian Ocean.

During our first Soular Disc pilgrimage to Egypt, we'd directly experienced that healing can only come about through the acknowledgement, inclusion and integration of our own inner shadow. Seeking to exclude this intrinsic part of our humanity, as we had discovered in Egypt, only serves to polarize our experiences further.

As the Chinese master geomancers understood and encoded in their famous symbol for yin and yang, the light intrinsic to physicalized consciousness cannot exist without shadow and the shadow cannot exist without light. The brightest light contains the seed of shadow, and within the deepest shadow, the seed of light glows.

We can choose to continue to express the extremes of these polarities or we can choose to heal and integrate. My good friend Kelly, who, like me, loves playing with the energy of words, calls this 'into-great' – our way through to the innate greatness of our being.

Each thought, word and deed is energy. Our 'e-motions' are energy in motion. Consequently, the more profound the emotion, whatever its essence, the more energetically powerful it is. Humanity's inter-related resonance with the energy field of Gaia means that the imprints of human emotions are held in the fabric of the Earth herself. Our human emotional memory thus remains within the landscape until dispersed or otherwise altered. We sense such energetic imprints in the 'atmosphere' of places where events incurring powerful emotions have happened, such as the trauma of battlefields. The geology of places, especially where there is a high incidence of quartz and geological faulting, such as the Great Rift Valley, and the interplay of water both below and above the ground play significant roles in the memory of this imprinting.

As I attuned to our forthcoming journey, I marvelled at the geological scale of this African Rift, which, at 4,000 miles long, is the largest overland fault line on Earth. The spreading of the Earth's tectonic plates, which continues today, gave rise to the geological tensions that birthed it. The scars of massive eruptions and earthquakes have necklaced the Rift's path with volcanoes and lakes – the elemental energies of Fire and Water. It is not surprising, then, that it holds the accumulation of our human energetic rifts.

I felt that any healing which our pilgrimage could be in service to and help bring about would reverberate at profound and collective levels.

*****

Our journey to Africa was organized by Stuart and Audrey Gedrim, and with John unable to be with us on this trip, his wife Ann joined our group.

Our itinerary began with the sacred sites of the area around Johannesburg and, following two days at bush camp in the Kruger National Park, we intended to travel to Zimbabwe for the eclipse. From there, we were to fly to Cape Town to complete our journey by connecting with and activating the Soular Disc at Table Mountain.

Several days before leaving for Africa, I facilitated a day's workshop on Mayan and Incan wisdom teachings, not realizing the imminent synchronicity and opportunity to empower our group intention.

The next morning, two Mayan shamans arrived on my doorstep! They told me that they had been guided to work with the energies of solar eclipses around the world, beginning in their homeland of Mexico in 1991. They were now intending to do the same during the solar eclipse in Africa – could I help them get there?

I immediately phoned Audrey and Stuart and gave them the glad tidings that we had two more people joining us. A slight matter of their having no money needed resolving, but with the empowerment of everyone's positive intention, in Europe and Africa, that's what, between us, we managed to achieve.

*****

I felt it would be a wonderful beginning to our African pilgrimage if we were able to meet Vusamazulu Credo Mutwa, the only surviving *sanusi*, the peak of the African shamanic tradition.

Credo is a renowned storyteller and historian of his people, having written *Indaba, my Children*, which tells the stories and legends of tribal life. His book, *Song of the Stars: The Lore of a Zulu Shaman*, shares the secret star lore of indigenous black Africans and tells of their ancient and ongoing extraterrestrial contacts.

While I felt inspired to meet Credo, Audrey and Stuart appeared very doubtful whether it would be possible and so I let go of the outcome. Only on arriving in Johannesburg did we realize that they had accomplished a miracle and not only were we going to meet Credo but we would be spending our first day and night at his newly opened retreat centre Naledi, which means 'Bright star'.

I also discovered why Audrey and Stuart had not seemed to encourage my request to meet Credo. They had worked harmoniously together for years, but then someone had told Credo untruths about them. Sadly, in the historical climate of South Africa, such tales had credibility and their friendship had been severed. But asking for us to meet Credo gave Stuart an opportunity to speak to him once more. They met again the day before our group arrived and rekindled their friendship.

So our journey of healing had already begun.

We were able to spend several hours with Credo, and the following morning, before we journeyed on, he and his companion, Virginia, also honoured us with a heartfelt and powerful blessing ceremony.

*****

Our next destination was the magnificent Blyde river canyon region of Mpumalanga, where we would acclimatize ourselves to the energies of the sacred sites there.

As we shaded our eyes in the bright sunlight at our first stop, we could see above us a bare hillside scattered with boulders. Stuart explained that this was an ancient site known as the Nomkumbulwanas stones and that every stone was reputed to connect with a star system.

As we walked up the hillside, we too began to quietly scatter, each of us drawn to a different part of the hillside and to a different stone. I found myself walking in a reverie to a cluster of large boulders near the summit of the hill where a gnarled thorn tree emerged from the centre of this ancient tableau.

As I clambered onto the flat surface of the largest stone and looked past the tree, I suddenly saw the sky filled with gem-coloured stars – and this was the middle of the day! I closed my eyes and still saw the stars. Emerald, garnet, aquamarine, citrine, sapphire and colours that seemed to stretch beyond the threshold of visible light shone with a richness so intense that I felt I could reach out and hold them in my hand.

Credo had told us that his people, the Zulu nation, believed that we were children of the stars. Now, as I stood lost in wonder, this became real for me at a profoundly new level. When we all came together again, from the looks on our faces, it was clear that I wasn't the only one to have experienced this powerful connection.

Re-membering our cosmic heritage was beginning to emerge as a crucial element in the healing theme of our journeys. Here it had arisen as we had connected with the stars, supported by Credo's calm acceptance of continuing extraterrestrial contact with humanity.

But I felt that these experiences were merely way-showers to deeper revelations yet to come.

*****

That afternoon in the Blyde river canyon, the conjunction of the Treur and Blyde rivers was a wonderful celebration of tumbling and surging waters. Off came shoes and socks as we all laughed and danced in the crystal-clear pools.

Sitting on the bank, Stuart then told us the story of the two rivers:

> In 1840, in the early days of European exploration of southern Africa, a wagon train of families arrived in this area. A party of their menfolk then left to forge a path through the mosquito-infested Lowveld to Mozambique in search of a route to the coast. Their women and children remained behind in the cool and healthy heights to await their return.
>
> That time came and long passed. After the disasters which had befallen other trekkers on the route to the

coast, as day followed day with no sign, the waiting women and children became ever more despondent. The Treur river – the river of sorrow – on which they were camped is named for this time of desperation.

Finally, when all hope was lost, the women reluctantly began to set out for home. But as they wearily prepared to ford the second river, they were overtaken by their men, who had returned after a heroic and successful journey. From then on the river became known as the Blyde, or the river of joy, in celebration of the menfolk's safe return.

Once again we were being shown the interplay of polarities that flow though our experience of what it is to be human. And again I pondered on their re-soulution and the nature of the third aspect of the cosmic trinity, through which all phenomena and all experience are ultimately co-created.

*****

It was the following day, as I gazed on the beauty of the Three Rondavels, a rock formation that expresses a trinity of energies embodying the essence of male, female and child, that my eyes were fully opened.

This cosmic trinity of mother, father and child is at the heart of many spiritual and metaphysical traditions. When we talk metaphysically about balance, however, we most often perceive it as that of the male and female polarity principles that pervade the Cosmos – the yin and yang of the Taoist teachings. Yet, as we'd begun to understand and directly experience in Egypt, the child needs to be an equal partner in our inner healing. And in the awakening energies of the 8th chakra of the universal heart, the energies of the heart, mind and will need to be in communion for this portal to our higher awareness to be activated.

Credo had shared with us that the ancient African spiritual traditions too had recognized this cosmic trinity. He and other spiritual elders say that this is a time when we can come together collectively by allowing our children and the inner child within each of us to guide our way.

As Credo says:

> *There are many nations in this world*
> *Under the shadow of that Sun.*
> *They are nations of many colours*
> *But they have one beating heart.*
> *They are all born of women.*
> *They all know the almighty God.*
> *They are all looking for love.*
> *Because they have One heart.*

*****

Travelling onwards, we arrived at Kruger National Park.

The game parks in South Africa make it clear that the animals there are the residents and the humans the tolerated visitors. This respect was further demonstrated while we were in Africa by an initiative of the South African government. Following an agreement with neighbouring countries, the borders were to be opened again after many years to allow the herds of animals to follow their ancient migration routes once more without restriction.

We all felt a sense of childlike excitement as we drove to our bush camp at Biyamiti, where we were warmly welcomed. During the next two days, as we explored the park, we were blessed to see at close quarters four of the 'big five' animals of Kruger. The elephant, lion, rhino, buffalo and leopard are the magnificent animals that every visitor to Kruger wants to see. To experience at close quarters a young bull elephant foraging from the upper branches of an acacia tree or the sudden charge – away from us thankfully – of an adult rhino is an unforgettable joy.

One evening, as we were driving back to camp, on the road ahead of us was an amazing sight: a huge eagle owl. As we slowed to a crawl, the magnificent bird spread his wings as if about to fly.

Now we were within feet of him and still he stayed.

We were in awe. We held our breath. Time stopped.

And as we gratefully watched, he majestically took flight, his powerful wings beating silently, taking him into the night.

The omen of the eagle owl reminded me that in shamanic traditions the eagle represents our connection with the divine, being both of the realm of Spirit and of Earth. In some traditions, the owl is known as the night eagle and again embodies the wisdom of embracing both light and shadow.

During that drive and the next morning we also saw three leopards. One of us had envisioned our experience of these magical creatures before we had seen them. Of all the big cats, leopards have had a special place in the priestly and shamanic activities of Africa. And from ancient times African priests have worn leopard skins as a mark of their initiatory authority.

Seeing the three leopards would prove significant, as the trinity is not only the embodiment of the cosmic principles of mother, father and child, but also the number of initiation in many cultures. The three elements in the process of inner transformation represent the intention, the intuition (inner-tuition) and the integration of learning that an initiation entails.

As the omens of the eagle owl and the leopards came together, what initiation of embracing the light and shadow awaited us during the coming time of the cosmic light and shadow of the solar eclipse?

*****

Reluctantly leaving the haven of Kruger, we journeyed on to Johannesburg. Here we were to meet up with some newly arriving members of our group, including our two Mayan friends, to travel together to Zimbabwe for our appointment with the solar eclipse.

The ancient Mayans were masters of space-time. Their understanding of the cycles of the Sun, Moon and Earth and of the visible planets, especially Venus, was profound. It felt utterly right that their descendants were with us to experience one of the greatest displays of cosmic harmony visible on Earth.

The Sun is 400 times larger than the Moon. Yet it is also 400 times further away from the Earth. This exact correlation, whose chance of arising coincidentally is literally astronomical, creates the miracle of a total eclipse.

*****

On the morning of the eclipse I woke up in the chill light of pre-dawn. I had arranged with the hotel to give us wake-up calls, but immediately had a foreboding that no one was going to be called. I dressed quickly and on my way to breakfast was assured by one of the hotel staff that the calls had been made.

We soon found out that they hadn't.

Stuart had woken up with the same premonition. Between us we managed to get everyone up, but the day started as it was destined to continue – in chaos.

*****

We'd arranged a pleasant two-hour drive to a site near a waterfall, a beautiful and gentle place at which to experience the eclipse. We were accompanied on the journey by a police car whose officers supposedly knew the way.

Three hours later, we were beginning to become concerned.

After four hours more so. After five, definitely.

We were all, however, sensing an underlying purpose to being 'lost' – which is what the bus driver and his attendants eventually admitted we were.

After six hours, we pulled up in the grounds of a school not far from the Mozambique border. There was a general agreement that wherever we were, this was going to be where we stayed and experienced the eclipse!

It proved to be the perfect place.

An amazingly varied community of people came together. Children and teachers from the school joined us and, as word rapidly spread, so did adults from the local village.

The two Mayans in our group were now dressed in their finery and preparing, with great love and care, to perform the ceremony of welcome and gratitude for the new beginning offered by the eclipse. In a less flamboyant way, the rest of us were also preparing to connect with the powerful energies of the eclipse in service to a common intention of facilitating healing and peace.

That the solar eclipse was taking place at the solstice felt greatly significant. The winter solstice in the southern hemisphere marks the energetic birth of a new year, and so the path of totality of the eclipse energized a new beginning.

*****

As the time of the eclipse approached, the bustle died down. Each group who had travelled so far for these few precious and unique moments prepared themselves and we became quiet and focused on the intention of our coming together.

We joined in a circle, purposefully creating a sacred space at this sacred time of cosmic communion. With hearts open, individually and together, we focused our thoughts and feelings on healing all rifts within ourselves and allowed that sense of wholeness to ripple outwards with unconditional love.

At 3.12 P.M. the two minutes of the total eclipse of the Sun would begin. As our watches counted down the remaining moments, we became aware that the bright afternoon light was fading. Through eclipse goggles we watched intently as the disc of the Moon began to cover that of the Sun.

Inexorably, more and more of the Sun was covered, the birds stopped singing and began to roost and a profound silence fell. In a cloudless sky, the miracle was realized as the eclipse became total and our world fell into shadow.

Standing in the awesome depths of the eclipse, I felt a deep sadness for the rifts our human family had experienced and a heartfelt hope that the seeds of healing would begin to germinate in the womb of this silent darkness.

Suddenly a dazzling flash of sunlight appeared as the Moon's journey continued on. Light returned and with it I felt a huge upsurge of joy, overspilling with tears of gratitude.

As the two Mayans in their spectacular costumes of feathers and shells began to dance their ceremony of celebration, dozens of local villagers gathered round to watch. At first they shyly hung back but the natural curiosity of the children drew them forward as looks of uncertainty gave way to smiles of pleasure. With the return of the Sun, we all joined in a great circle around the two dancers in celebration of what we had all experienced. African songs gave way to applause and laughter, which flowed into more songs, until the bus driver and our escort were telling us that it was time to leave.

*****

In talking with the local people, our euphoria was saddened by the realization of how devastating the AIDS epidemic was in Africa. To see babies already suffering from AIDS lying in the arms of their mothers was to fully appreciate its ravages – an everyday, shocking reality. We realized that not only would those mothers not live to see their children grow up, but that the children themselves were likely to die before adulthood.

We promised to keep in touch, to return if possible and to help in any practical way we could. That day every one of us gained a deeper awareness of the physical fragility and the inner strength of our human family that even within an abyss of pain still has an incredible capacity for joy.

*****

As we bumped along on the six-hour drive back to Harare the late afternoon quickly slipped into night, and the chatter of sharing our experiences gave way to quiet reflection.

My heart called me to Avebury where I knew many of our friends were readying for one of the global meditations we had come to call the rainbow bridges. My friend Chris Waters and I had organized these solsticial meditations there since 1997, when several hundred people had participated in a peace meditation to co-create a bridge – as the Native American elders had prophesied – between the rainbow tribes of the Earth.

As the moment for the rainbow bridge meditation arrived, Brian and I merged our unconditionally loving intention for healing within the exponential power of the group prayers around the world and I felt a deep peace gently wash through me.

*****

Next day the loud pre-dawn knocks on our doors emphasized that the hotel staff were determined to make up for the previous morning. Even so, we cut it fine in arriving at the airport for our flight to Jo'burg and our connecting flight to Cape Town. Waiting bleary-eyed at the back of a longish queue at check-in, I had no conscious awareness of the drama about to unfold.

Harare International Airport had just opened to cater for the large number of visitors expected for the eclipse. Despite its appearance as a brand-new high-tech facility, staff training didn't appear to have been a significant part of the planning.

When we finally arrived at the front of the queue and some of us had already managed to obtain precious boarding cards, we were told that there wasn't room for all of us on the flight.

It's probably best to draw a veil over the next hour or so. Suffice to say that after being told repeated untruths by airport staff, losing three of our group onto the flight we should all have been on, not being allowed to get them off that flight so we could all stay together and not being able to tell them what was going on – well, Stuart and I lost it!

As one part of myself was in the throes of this drama, fuelled by a frustrated feeling of responsibility and concern, I could sense another part was witnessing it all, smiling and knowing that all was well.

Finally, the airport manager, a competent and kindly woman, agreed to get us on the next flight. As we walked through customs, a harassed official asked in a weary voice, 'You *are* leaving, aren't you?'

Both amused and sad, I appreciated how systems and institutions can overwhelm us.

The drama had been a big lesson in communication and also when to stand firm and when to let go. In the unfolding turmoil I could have chosen to remain calm, could have listened and accepted the situation earlier and could have trusted that all was well. . . .

The remainder of the day continued as it had begun, with us missing our connecting flight and Stuart's case being lost in transit. Ah well. By this point I had reached a state of eerie calm and, thank goodness, regained my sense of humour!

We finally made it to our hotel in Cape Town, to be greeted by our 'lost' three who had enjoyed an uneventful journey and had been relaxing while awaiting our arrival.

Later, as I mulled over our dance of order and chaos, light and shadow, I remembered the omen of the eagle owl and its message of embracing light and shadow.

A great truism is that we experience the world forwards and understand it backwards! The understanding we gain can, however, guide us forward – and so the co-creative dance of consciousness continues to flow.

*****

Dean Liprini is a spiritual seeker and geomancer who from boyhood has been receiving guidance in rediscovering an alignment of sacred sites in South Africa. What Dean terms 'the Pathway of the Sun' is an ancient 500-mile long alignment of megalithic stone observatories which track the cardinal directions of the Sun at the solstices and equinoxes from what is now Cape Town in the west to Port Elizabeth in the east.

Dean has discovered that for each observatory, the rock from which it is formed either naturally takes the shape of a human face or has been sculpted to this effect, often with holes where the eyes are. As part of this geomantic grid, there are also marker stones, which he believes were positioned to align with the Moon and stars.

At many of the observatories Dean has also discovered light effects designed to be reflected in the water of adjacent sacred pools. As he has noted, where these light paths enter or exit, they form gateways of the Sun, guarded by huge stone gatekeepers, watchmen which are symbolically awakened or put to sleep by the first and last rays of the rising and setting Sun.

Dean has walked the pathway over many years. For him, this is a passionate inner as well as outer journey of continuing discovery.

As we arrived to connect energetically with and activate the Soular Disc, Dean was preparing to publicly share his private understanding and has since authored the book of his discovery, *Pathways of the Sun*. As he took us to some of the sacred sites in the Cape Town area, his excitement and respect for the people who had created this vast landscape geometry were contagious.

The Elohim had guided me months before that the Soular Disc was 'at Table Mountain', the flat-topped mountain which overlooks Cape Town. However, until our arrival I hadn't appreciated how huge the mountain is, or received confirmation as to where exactly the Disc's energies were centred.

While I'd felt that in some way the Pathway of the Sun would be very important in connection with the location of the Soular Disc, I hadn't spoken to Dean or received any prior information of his discoveries. Stuart and Audrey had been intimately involved in his work for a number of years, but had considered that I needed to speak to him directly.

What was about to unfold made me weep with gratitude.

*****

We were led to a beautiful vantage-point overlooking Cape Town, with a wonderful view of Table Mountain. As we climbed, Dean pointed out another peak rising alongside Table Mountain, the two being separated by a narrow valley.

When we heard that this peak, with its distinctive leonine shape, was called the Lion's Head, I suddenly realized that Table Mountain, with its flat top and pyramidal shape, and the peak of the Lion's Head at the southern tip of Africa reflect the Great Pyramid and Sphinx at the northern tip of the continent. Each of them energetically anchors the Rift and both are essential to releasing and rebalancing its energies.

I now understood why our first journey had been to Egypt and why this journey to Africa was the second.

When Dean then mentioned that the western portal of the Pathway of the Sun was on the slopes of Table Mountain, between it and the Lion's Head, I knew that was where the epicentre of the Disc's energies was located – and why the Elohim had stressed that it was *at* Table Mountain and not *on* it.

Dean also told us that this portal aligned with and was energized by the sunrise at the winter solstice. The guidance of the Elohim had been to activate the Soular Disc on 24 June, the third day after the solar eclipse. At the time of the solstices, the Sun rises at the same place on the horizon for three days; at any other time of the year, it journeys daily farther to the north or south.

Our timing of activating the Soular Disc energized by the solar eclipse, then, lay at the culmination of the creative energies of the winter solstice sunrise to which the Disc's portal was aligned and the day the Sun's cosmic cycle began anew.

Everything had finally fallen into place!

*****

Joined by some local friends of Stuart and Audrey and surrounded by a thick mist, we climbed the slopes of Table Mountain to the portal. As we silently followed each other up the narrow path, everything around us was very still.

Ahead of us, eerily emerging from the mist, I saw two great rocks standing at right angles to each other, intentionally placed there, and realized that the natural slope of the mountain rose to form the third side of the portal, open to the solstice sunrise. One of the huge rocks was a rounded female shape, embodying the essence of yin energy, while the other was taller and embodied yang or male energy.

I sensed that the three sides of the trinity portal, the two great stones and the hillside itself formed both a physical and energetic grail. Arthurian legends talk of the search for the Holy Grail, the cup said to have held the blood of the Master Jesus. Metaphysical teachings understand that the grail is in the heart too – that when we embrace Spirit and all that we are with unconditional love, at that moment we become unity or christed consciousness. I now began to see that the Soular Discs were such planetary grails.

Forming a circle that included the two great portal stones, we stood together, voicing our prayers for healing the rifts of fear and separation. As the Fire of our spirits embraced the Water of our emotions and the watery mist around us resonated with the alchemical transformation of love, the activation of the Disc was complete.

*****

As I voiced my personal prayer for healing the rifts of our human family, I recalled that every single one of the more than six billion people living on Earth today was descended from a small group of anatomically modern humans who lived in Africa between 150,000 and 200,000 years ago. Tracing back key aspects of our genetic lineage such as the mitochondrial DNA passed down the female line and the Y chromosome passed through the male strongly suggests that this original group may only have totalled a few thousand people. Since then, what we identify in our modern global population as ethnic characteristics, including skin colour, has evolved from the differentiation of only a few nucleotides, the building blocks of the DNA molecule, amongst the billions comprising our human DNA. Our apparent ethnic diversity is truly only skin-deep, and the richness of our behavioural characteristics is overwhelmingly derived from a combination of our cultural heritage, our individual personalities and the circumstances of our life's journey.

Nowhere else on Earth is the amazing expression of human life as diverse as in Africa. Its human story, too, spans the entire length of our collective journey; and its tribes, races and religions embrace all colours and creeds.

If we can learn here to celebrate, rather than fear, such diversity and recognize the underlying unity that births its creative abundance, we can surely begin to heal the rifts which have divided us all for so long.

*****

The beginnings of our human heritage are rooted in Africa. And here I began to directly experience the grounding of my own energies through a 9th chakra approximately six inches below my feet. I could powerfully feel how this chakra enabled the integration and physical grounding of the energies of the 8th chakra of the universal heart and the higher transpersonal chakras that we are progressively realizing are now accessible to us.

Our traditional root chakra is sufficient to ground our personal energies. However, as we continued to discover, grounding or releasing energies through the vortex of this 9th – or earthstar – chakra enables us to re-member our terrestrial lineage and commune with Gaia, the living Earth, and the children of all her many realms.

*****

As we said our farewells, Dean gave me a pure quartz crystal from the western gateway of the Pathway of the Sun and I knew it was to go with me on our next journey to connect with the Soular Disc in the far west of China.

As I held it in the palm of my hand, I felt an ancient memory stirring within me that seemed to spiral back like the double helix of the DNA chain to the origins of our human journey.

In China, we were to gain a deeper understanding of our hidden history and uncover shocking revelations of our extraterrestrial heritage.

☷ ☼ ☷

CHAPTER 3
China

CHAPTER 3

CHINA
August 2001

Back in England for the short time before journeying on to China, I began to sense that the inner healing facilitated by the Soular Discs would require us to re-member the wholeness of who we *really* are – individually and collectively.

And I somehow knew that this would need us to acknowledge and understand not only our human but also our extraterrestrial heritage.

*****

Ancient Sumerian myths refer to a race of extraterrestrial reptilian beings, the Annunaki, arriving on Earth from their home planet, Nibiru, in the outer reaches of our Soular System. Research into the myths, together with channelled and guided information, suggests that they were here initially to mine for gold, which was apparently needed to stabilize the Nibiruan atmosphere that was degrading dangerously.

Though initially carrying out the mining themselves, at some point the Annunaki decided to create the race of human beings to carry out the hard labour of extracting the gold. Both the Sumerian myths and the Bible reference the mating of such 'gods', with the 'daughters of men', and researchers have considered this to be a genetic modification of hominids some 200 millennia ago to form modern humans.

The recent genome project that has traced our collective ancestry back through our mitochondrial DNA to a very few 'Eves' in this same time-frame lends additional support to these ancient myths.

The two leaders of the reptilian Annunaki are referred to as the brothers Enki and Enlil. And each had a very different agenda for this genetic modification of humanity. Enlil's agenda was the creation of a slave race, whereas Enki's was ultimately to manifest the enormous potential embodied in the hybrid human-Annunaki being – including the physical embodiment of emotion, which we humans fully express and which it appears the Annunaki cannot.

This energetic as well as physical dynamic also perhaps helps to explain a deep rift within our psyche. For the part of us that embodies the Enki energy knows we are divine beings, eternal and extraordinary spirits and vastly more than our human experience. But another part of our psyche resonates with the Enlil agenda and is expressed in the deep fears and feelings of worthlessness that so often dis-empower us.

In the ancient past perhaps our ancestors saw with their own eyes the Annunaki dragons walking the Earth. Over millennia, the memories of their encounters have become myth and legend. Yet the myriad of such legends and folk memories of dragons from all around the world continues to testify to a powerful influence.

Many ancient traditions tell of benevolent dragon-like beings bringing the benefits of civilization, while others reveal the manipulative control of dragon rulers. In the Bible, Enki is personified as the serpent in the Garden of Eden, encouraging Eve and, through her, Adam to eat of the Tree of Knowledge. Throughout South American legends the winged serpents Kulkulkan and Quetzalcoatl are likewise bringers of wisdom, and many of the earliest rulers and dynastic lineages are described as the sons of dragons. And now a growing number of researchers are maintaining that a hidden Enlil agenda lies behind millennia-long attempts to control human destiny by instilling fear and presenting ostensible solutions that support its covert aims.

Now, as we awake from a collective amnesia, is it time for this 'hidden' history and perception of the continuing Annunaki involvement with humanity to emerge into our awareness and for our psyche to be reconciled and healed?

The answers were to be revealed to us as we journeyed in China.

*****

The Elohim were clear that we were to go to China in August. And given my understanding that the Soular Disc was located at the ancient stupa of Rawak in north-western China, in the region of the Takla Makan desert and Tarim Basin, this would be our primary focus.

As the second lowest land area in the world, this region has seen summer temperatures of well over 120° Fahrenheit. Knowing that our final journey to the Disc involved walking through the desert, all I could do was to reassure John (and myself) that the guidance had been that we would be well protected!

From time immemorial this region, which the age-old Silk Road traverses, has birthed legends, including those of mysterious Shambhala, a spiritual sanctuary of universal wisdom and peace.

Sacred to Hindus, Buddhists and Moslems alike, the basin is bounded on the south by the Kunlun mountain range separating it from the Tibetan plateau and on the north by the Tien Shen range, which extends into the desolate landscape of Mongolia.

It is in the Kunlun mountains that a portal to Shambhala is said to open for those enlightened ones who seek to be in its service. It was here, over two millennia ago, that the Chinese sage Lao

Tzu was said to be travelling when he left his followers, never to return.

Geomantically, the basin also forms a powerful planetary grail, profoundly resonant with the heart energy of Quan Yin, 'the Lady of the West', the Chinese goddess of compassion, whose guiding presence I now began to sense.

At the heart of this grail is an ancient ruined Buddhist stupa at Rawak. It is this high tower that local legends prophesy will be the place of the coming manifestation of the Maitreya Buddha. This was our destination, as it was here that the Elohim had told me that the 3rd Soular Disc was located.

*****

Arriving in Beijing after long journeys from Europe and America, our group gathered and took time to settle and get to know each other. This time we were small in number, but as we introduced ourselves, the fact that most of us had a long-time fascination with or direct experience of extraterrestrial contact now came as no surprise.

Before journeying on to the Takla Makan Basin, we had arranged to spend a couple of days in Beijing, where we energetically connected with the Altar of Earth and the Temple of Heaven.

The Altar of Earth is located in what is now a peaceful park in the city. No one paid any attention to us as we formed a circle and each spoke of our intentions for the journey to come and asked that they be well grounded through us.

In contrast, Tiantan, the Temple of Heaven, is a complex of temples and altars which for the five centuries before the Chinese Revolution of 1911 was the centre of imperial ceremonial. Reflecting the Chinese energetic perception of Heaven as circular and Earth as square, the circular temples and altars are built on square bases and the entire complex forms a semi-circle which sits inside a square.

The ancient Chinese saw China as the Middle Kingdom, the balance between Heaven and Earth. Each year at the winter solstice the Emperor would ceremoniously celebrate this meeting of cosmic energies and pray for their continuing sustenance of the Middle Kingdom.

In attuning ourselves to the energies of the Temple of Heaven, we invited them to flow through us and consciously reconciled the energies of Heaven and Earth within ourselves. Dedicating ourselves individually and our group as a whole to the journey ahead, we asked for the blessing and gentle guidance of Quan Yin to be with us.

We also took time to visit the nearby Forbidden City, the huge enclave that was home to the Emperor and the imperial Chinese court. As we wandered round, I noticed how it was constructed exactly in harmony with the principles of *feng shui* in order to energetically balance the cosmic female and male principles, yin and yang. Positioned at the centre of China, its purpose was also to ensure that the rule of the Emperor, known as 'the Son of Heaven', would be continually recreated from here and always prevail.

*****

We were fascinated to discover that Chinese legend tells of the human race beginning with the goddess Nu Kua, who was half-human and half-dragon. And the Emperor, embodying these cosmic powers, was known as 'the Son of the Dragon'.

The Emperor's symbol, the dragon, is seen throughout the Forbidden City. But while we could see these outer images of the dragon, within myself I was also beginning to strongly feel the presence of the dragon energy of Enlil.

Reflecting on these powerful connections, I recalled that in Chinese astrology, of the 12 zodiac signs which describe human personalities, all but one are 'real' animals – the other is the dragon.

Those born in the year of the dragon are perceived as embodying power, charisma and self-belief – not always benignly. The dragon is appropriately a yang, or outgoing, sign, and wood is perceived as being its natural element. Wood, which is imbued with the creative growth and expression of life, naturally complements the dragon energies.

I now remembered too that I was born in a year of the dragon and that the full Chinese astrological cycle of 60 years would culminate for me in 2012.

On the macrocosmic scale of the Earth, the telluric lines that are the energetic veins and arteries of natural Earth energies are known in China as 'the lines of the dragon' and a master of geomantic *feng shui* is called a 'dragon man'. The dragon man follows or 'rides' the lines of the dragon to understand and enhance the flow of beneficial life-force and to deflect or drain the accumulation of the negative. Mountain tops are the traditional home of the dragon kings who control the weather, with the different dragon forms embodying the very life force or *ch'i*.

In the microcosm of the human body, balancing and enhancing the flow of *ch'i* through the energy meridians, the equivalent of the Earth's dragon lines, to eliminate dis-ease and promote well-being is accomplished through the equivalent technique of acupuncture.

We were surrounded and pervaded by dragon energies. In Beijing and throughout our journey we were to experience directly how China continually pays homage to the dragon and how both the Annunaki agendas of Enlil and Enki, of enslavement and cosmic potential, permeate its landscape and culture.

*****

Leaving Beijing, we flew on to Urumji in the Tarim Basin. Arriving late at night and tired from our flight, we still couldn't resist the hotel shop, still open at this hour.

Rare white jade is washed down in the rivers from the Kunlun mountains. And as I stood in the shop, I felt that a statue of Quan Yin sculpted from this pure and beautiful stone would be an ever-present and powerful presence in our journey. As I looked up, I saw her, radiant and tranquil, gazing at me.

Safe in her travelling box, our Quan Yin did indeed bless us every day.

Elsewhere in the shop, I saw vibrant pieces of flaming red coral found in the desert. In Africa, one of our group, Christine, had had an insight that the Soular Discs were elementally resonant with Fire and Water. Now this fire-like reminder that the desert that now surrounds the Disc at Rawak was once a sea made me smile.

It felt right to connect physically with the Water element here and the next day we travelled into the nearby mountains to see the Heavenly Lake. We felt guided to connect the energies of the lake with those at Rawak. After enjoying a boat cruise on the lake, surrounded by the many others visiting this lovely place, we managed to find a quiet spot for our attunement.

In summer, the bare mountain ridges around the lake are sinuously redolent of dragons, and as we attuned to their elemental energies, the image of a golden dragon immediately came forward. Understanding its message, however, took longer and unfolded as we journeyed on.

After our meditation, we filled a small bottle with lake water to take with us. Energetically and physically, it would bring the element of Water to balance that of the elemental Fire of the desert now surrounding the Rawak Disc.

*****

Before leaving Urumji, we found time to visit the local museum, where the nearly 4,000-year-old mummy named 'the Beauty of Loulan' after the place she was discovered now sleeps.

Other mummies unearthed from beneath the desert sands – all of them tall and dignified – accompany her, each wearing intricate clothes of tartan and having wonderfully preserved faces tattooed with spirals. Appearing much more European than Asian, their presence here, so far from their homelands, remains an enigma.

As I explored the museum I was drawn to a tall stone statue, a brooding and powerful presence whose features were too worn to be seen clearly. As I discovered that it had been brought from Aksu, I felt the name reverberate deep in my memory.

Some years before, I'd experienced a vision of being one of the Annunaki, part of an ancient exploratory expedition led by Enki. I'd intuitively understood that we had been in the far west of what was now China, and had known without understanding how that far into the future the place would become known as Aksu. But I hadn't realized until now that there was actually a town by that name. Although we had no plans to go there, it seemed that doors from my ancient past were opening.

The next day we were to fly across the desert to the oasis of Hotan in the foothills of the Kunlun. Hearing that our flight was delayed enabled us to revisit the museum and me to connect with the Aksu statue at a deeper level. As I gazed at his deeply weathered face I had a sense that we would meet him, or an embodiment of his energy, once more on our journey, but how and where I didn't know.

Eventually arriving at the airport to catch our delayed flight, we were told that we would not be flying directly to Hotan but would be diverting instead to Aksu!

Our stop there was the briefest I've ever experienced during any stopover flight anywhere in the world – only enough time to literally stretch our legs and to stand momentarily on the ground of my ancient memory. I just knew that this was to enable me to connect powerfully with the Enki energy.

The energetic links were being made and I surrendered to the tapestry of purpose that was being woven around me.

*****

The people of Hotan are primarily Uighurs, the Central Asian tribe that researcher Charles Churchward considered to be a remnant of the ancient Lemurian people. These graceful and open-hearted folk are primarily Moslem and welcomed us kindly into their community.

The small town of Hotan is famous as a source of jade, which the two branches of the Hotan river, the Yorungkash and the Karakash, meaning 'White Jade' and 'Black Jade' in the Uighur language, wash down from the heights. These two rivers epitomize the embrace and reconciliation of light and shadow.

Jade is known as the dream stone, and it has been said that to fulfil our destiny, we must fulfil our dreams. As a stone of fidelity, it also brings the realization of our potential and rewards devotion to our higher purpose.

Carved in the form of deities, it is also deemed to offer protection and support to one's efforts, which was a further reminder to me of the loving presence of our white jade Quan Yin. It was she who would guide us as we left Hotan and travelled into the desert, initially by four-wheel-drive truck and then on foot, heading for the ruined Buddhist stupa at Rawak and the Soular Disc.

*****

In this hottest place in China, as promised by the Elohim we were well protected, with the morning of 23 August dawning cloudy and cool.

Deep in the desert, accompanied by a local government official deemed essential for our safety in this vast place of unmarked and undifferentiated sand dunes, we left our vehicle and walked slowly on, our heads bowed against the windblown sand. Ahead, the ancient stupa of Rawak, one of the most ancient Buddhist holy places in China, towered above us.

Inexorably, year by year, the desert has encroached on this once vibrant and fertile region. Now ruined and desolate, it is nevertheless the place where local legend says that the coming Maitreya Buddha, the next incarnation of Buddhic consciousness, will manifest.

At the stupa, as we settled ourselves into a circle and quietened our minds to connect with the energies of the Soular Disc, I began by attuning myself to the vibration of my 8th chakra. As I felt this portal to my higher awareness energetically open, I sent a beam of energy down through the earthstar chakra beneath my feet and deep into the very heart of Gaia. I felt the returning pulse of Gaia flow through me and continue up to the 10th chakra, above my head, a chakra that I was now beginning to be able to access within my expanded transpersonal energy field. I was discovering that this newly accessible chakra connects us energetically with the matrix of consciousness that is our Soular System.

Immediately an image came into my inner vision and I offered myself up to the experience of its message.

*****

I saw the original coming of the Annunaki to Earth and, having connected with both the Enlil and Enki energies during our journey, could now sense their intentions of so long ago.

I saw the Annunaki, few in number, toiling in the mines they had delved deep into the Earth for what seemed liked millennia. I could feel their urgent and continuing need for gold alongside their frustration and their tiring of the seemingly endless hard labour. I then sensed their relief and excitement as they saw an opportunity for respite by genetically manipulating the early humans of the planet to create a slave race. This was the agenda of Enlil.

As these images flowed through my mind, I saw how Enki, as the leading scientist of his race, took on the responsibility for carrying out this programme of manipulation. I sensed too his realization of the possibility of the physical embodiment of a higher destiny as he came to understand the emotional and mental potential of humanity.

His agenda, in contrast to Enlil's, recognized that a human-Annunaki hybrid could embody emotional feeling and the passion of creativity at a level inaccessible to the Annunaki themselves.

*****

While energetically I'd been directly aware of Enki since the journey to Egypt two years before and the reactivation of the Enki/Encke shield, I'd been unwilling to connect to the Enlil energy. My own judgement of his intention to control humanity had for years imprisoned my perception of him. Now, as I attuned to his energy without judgement, I could see through his eyes and sense his motivation. For the first time I understood that he was, in his own way, seeking to save his people – but without any awareness of, or regard for, the consequences for us, his human slaves.

But now, in my inner vision, I could vividly see Enki and Enlil, after many millennia of separation, approaching each other from what seemed to be a vast distance. They came together until at last they embraced.

As I opened myself to a yet deeper understanding, I could feel within me their two polarized energies coming together – a beginning of the reconciliation of a rift as old as humanity. In that moment of integration and forgiveness, I knew that the 3rd Soular Disc had been activated.

Suddenly the golden dragon we had first encountered at the Heavenly Lake took on the energy of Enlil, the expression of his higher self.

Later, we also came to understand that the essence of the Maitreya Buddha embodied the higher self of Enki, the culmination of his ancient agenda for us, the human-Annunaki race.

It was perfect that the reconciliation of Enki and Enlil began at Rawak, where it is said that the returning Maitreya Buddha will manifest.

*****

Aware that I still had the crystal gifted to me by Dean in Africa, I knew that I needed to leave it within the stupa.

The government official with us was very unwilling to allow us access until I mentioned that I was an archaeologist. He was still completely unmoved by my request for us all to gain entry, but did allow me to clamber up the stupa's walls and drop down into the sole chamber we had seen from far below.

As I crouched in its narrow sandblown interior, I offered a prayer of gratitude for all we had experienced and for all that was still to come. I reached as far into the chamber as I could, leaving the crystal from the Pathway of the Sun to act as a rainbow bridge of healing intention.

Becoming concerned that the official had asked me to stay in the stupa for only a short time, I quickly reached down and clasped in my palm a small stone from the floor of the chamber. This was to be taken with me as the link to the next Soular Disc in Antarctica. Holding it tightly and without looking at it, I scrambled out and down to rejoin my companions.

Back with the others, I opened my hand to take a look at the stone. Within it, a grey face looked back at me, long with a pointed chin, tiny mouth and large eyes – the archetypal face of so many extraterrestrial encounters.

*****

The energetic reconciliation of Enki and Enlil reverberated as we journeyed onwards to Xi'an and the terracotta army of the Emperor Qinshihuang, the founder and creator of the Chinese Empire.

In 1974 three farming companions were digging a new well near Qinshihuang's mausoleum, just over 20 miles east of Xi'an, when they broke through the roof of a giant underground pit. The greatest archaeological discovery of modern times, described as the Eighth Wonder of the World, had been made.

The pyramidal shape of the mausoleum of Qinshihuang is precisely positioned in accordance with the principles of *feng shui*, with the Lishan mountain protecting it to the south and the Wei river flowing by to the north. Begun in 221 BC, taking 38 years to complete and conscripting at times nearly three-quarters of a million labourers, it is huge.

The historian Sima Qian describes Qin's burial chamber as being a microcosm of the empire, with mercury pumped in to represent rivers and the ocean, and the ceiling ornamented with precious stones to reflect the celestial bodies. He reports that on the Emperor's death his childless concubines accompanied him to the afterlife and all the artisans who had worked on the tomb were killed to prevent them divulging its secrets.

While the tumulus has been badly eroded over the last two millennia, the Emperor's burial chamber and treasures remain amazingly intact about 100 feet below ground.

Around the tumulus, a vast necropolis of more than 400 attendant burial pits and tombs has been identified, covering an area of over 22 square miles. Here lies the terracotta army of Emperor Qinshihuang.

Buried over two millennia ago and intended to remain there for eternity, the entombed terracotta warriors are life-sized representations of Qin's million-strong army. While the bodies of these nearly 7,000 soldiers, archers and horsemen are constructed from a number of patterned moulds, each sculpted face is individual and unique – and likely to have been modelled on the real soldiers of the army.

Together with chariots and terracotta horses, the warriors were armed with authentic bronze weapons – able and ready to battle Qin's enemies forever.

*****

As we walked around the massive pits housing the terracotta army, we came upon the statue of the general of Qin's army. Looking into his eyes, I saw the face of the ancient stone statue of Aksu looking back at me and suddenly recognized the embodied essence of the Enlil energy.

Ruling from the age of 13, Qin unified six independent kingdoms into a vast empire now known as China, and named after him. Controlling it with a rod of iron, he ensured that the dragon energy was embodied and enshrined within every aspect of its society. He is remembered as a ruthless tyrant who believed that human nature was innately bad and had to be restrained by draconian laws of state.

Intending that his empire should last for '10,000 years', Qin died during a fruitless quest to discover the fabled island of the immortals and the secret of longevity they reputedly possessed. Within a few years of his death, his empire disintegrated into civil war. Yet the dynasties that succeeded his continued the implacable rule of empire for two millennia.

At the heart of the imperium, Qin's mausoleum continues to anchor those energies to this day. Stretching beyond the horizon, across the landscape of the Wei river plain, are up to 100 further pyramid mausoleums of other dynasties, though none can compare in scale to Qin's. Together, they create a web of geomantic energy linking each dynasty to the continuation of China's power.

I now understood that the reconciliation of the Enlil and Enki energies would be in service to the balance and release of the over-controlling influence of the Enlil-inspired empire whose energies still rippled into the present day.

*****

Upon returning to Beijing, we enjoyed a quiet day exploring the havens of the Temple of Confucius and the Buddhist Temple.

The latter houses a huge array of statues of the Buddha in all his aspects. We had heard that a great statue of the Maitreya Buddha was here too and wished to offer our gratitude to him for all that the journey had revealed. As we came upon him in the gentle dimness of the temple, we couldn't believe our eyes. There at his feet, in this temple dedicated solely to the many aspects of the Buddha, was a white statue of Quan Yin, the very size of the one that accompanied us. What a wonderful validation of her guiding and compassionate presence throughout our journey and her spiritual connection with the Maitreya Buddha of Rawak.

*****

A few miles from the city is one of the few places where visitors can still walk along the Great Wall of China, built, according to historians, to keep so-called barbarians out of the empire. History relates that its construction depended on economic slavery as a means of paying the harsh and heavy taxes imposed by Qin, its initial instigator.

As we looked far into the distance, we could discern its sinuous path following the contours of the land and we could feel its powerful geomantic energies following a vast dragon line from the ocean to the far west of China, at its greatest extent nearly 6,000 miles long and ending only a couple of hundred miles from Rawak.

Having experienced the energies of the Emperor Qin, I now understood that not only was the Great Wall intended to keep barbarians out, but also, perhaps primarily, to enclose and protect the Enlil agenda and the energies of control embodied within the Chinese Empire. I smiled, as I sensed that the innate energies of the Soular Disc might have prevented the prospective completion of the Great Wall in the far west. It might thus have ensured that while the Emperor's dominance would control his own people, the empire would be unable to fully manifest its agenda of domination beyond its borders.

And with sudden insight, I now could sense that the energies of the Maitreya Buddha resonated with the wisdom and enlightened awareness of Enki.

Feeling the compassionate energies of Quan Yin at work here too, I reflected, with appreciation, on the many gifts of knowledge arising from the Enki aspects of the empire that the Chinese people had brought to the world over the millennia.

*****

We completed our journey where it began, in Beijing at the Temple of Heaven. Together in silent meditation we offered gratitude and prayers for the continuing purpose of the Soular Disc journeys. Then each of us separately made our way to a quiet place to reflect and offer thanks for our own personal experience and healing.

From our arrival in China, a plethora of posters had ensured that we were very aware that the Olympics of 2008 had just been awarded to the country. The Chinese Empire had long held itself aloof from the rest of the world, but now the iconic symbol of the Olympics seemed to embody the reconciliation which had been activated at Rawak.

The understanding that emerged during our journey and our connection with the 3rd Soular Disc revealed that now is the time not only for us to collectively perceive our 'hidden' history but also for us to recognize that we have the opportunity to go beyond judgement and to reconcile the Enki and Enlil energies within us.

Ultimately, the journey had offered me a profoundly felt opportunity to transcend judgement. For many years I had avoided associating with the Enlil aspect of the Annunaki energy, having judged its motivation. I now realized that I had been judging and condemning this aspect within myself. In accepting and to some extent understanding it, I was finally able to reconcile my own energetic resonance with the Annunaki. For the first time I began to feel wholly free of victim mentality – liberated from the energies of control and manipulation, either via projecting onto others or having them project onto me. I began to sense the 'em'powerment of such freedom – in contrast to the 'me'powerment of ego-based strength.

And I now sensed the beginning of the realization of the potential dreamed of by Enki.

*****

As the year drew to its close, I reflected on the profound changes brought about by the three journeys. We were realizing through direct experience that by denying or excluding aspects of ourselves we would rather not acknowledge, they would only persist, and had begun to understand that for our individual and collective healing we would have to embrace and reconcile all that we are. Only then would we be able to release the fears and traumas that separated us.

I was also grateful for the ways in which each journey had woven for us an exquisite tapestry offering us a growing understanding of our collective spiritual heritage, a profound appreciation of the realms of Gaia and an expanding awareness of the wider Cosmos.

And I appreciated how such understanding was inextricably connected to, and grounded within, our everyday human experience.

Those of us who were able to stay in regular contact began to work more closely together as the guidance of the Elohim continued to flow and our collective understanding continued to deepen. We explored how the energetic 12-into-13 harmonic of consciousness embodied in the 12 Discs related to our healing at a soular level and their link to the mysterious 13th master key.

Accessing the energies of the 10th chakra was also enabling me to expand my awareness of and connection with the archetypal energies of our Soular System.

Leading-edge science is now discovering that the Universe is an interrelated and conscious whole, a cosmic hologram energetically relating to itself at all scales and levels of experience. Astrologers have long understood that our Solar System is a self-relating hologram within which individuated and collective soul experience is played out. As I was now beginning to experience directly, at its most profound essence, our own Solar System of Sun, planets and myriad life forms is a Soular System of collective consciousness.

It is no accident that the ancient astrologers divided the sky into a 12-fold zodiac. Through the Sun, the Moon and the Earth, we may perceive the embodiment of the cosmic trinity – the solar male, the lunar female and the earthly child. The exquisite rhythm of their cycles also embodies the fundamental harmonic of 12 and 13. For in a solar year there are just over 12 full Moons and 13 sidereal months, where the path of the Moon is measured against the stellar background. In this harmonic dance of 12 and 13, are they showing us that we must also dance with the cosmic trinity of the male, female and child of our inner being to experience our own wholeness?

The ancient Sumerian myths refer to our Soular System as embodying 12 astronomical bodies – the Sun, Moon, Earth, eight other planets (including the outer planets not rediscovered for millennia) and an unknown 12th planet. The researcher Zecharia Sitchin describes how the myths portray the chaos caused as this planet, Nibiru, the home planet of the Annunaki, roamed through our Soular System bringing catastrophe and causing the formation of the asteroid belt.

The planetoid Chiron, which was only discovered in the 1970s, may be a remnant of this catastrophe. Energetically it is viewed by astrologers as bringing a deeper awareness of our inner wounding and facilitating its healing on individual and collective levels.

The old adage of 'seeing is believing' should perhaps be rephrased as 'believing is seeing'. Are we now seeing the dismembered debris of this ancient catastrophe as the 12th energetic element of our Soular System at the very point when we are ready to offer ourselves the opportunity to re-member and heal? And will the discovery of the 12th planet complete this process of re-membering?

As we progressively access the transpersonal chakras of our unity energy field, our journey into wholeness is also a journey for our entire Soular System, supported by the unconditionally loving energies of the Soular Discs. Now able to access the 10th chakra, we are re-membering our hidden history, enabling the Annunaki energies within us to be reconciled and allowing ourselves to gain an ever-greater awareness of our extraterrestrial heritage.

*****

As if to complete the next stage of our understanding, the reason why the Elohim had guided us to complete the journeys in early November 2003 was also revealed.

A friend called to ask whether I'd heard of the Harmonic Concordance. At that point, I hadn't. I learned that California-based astrologer Johnny Mirehiel had first identified this astronomical and astrological alignment, and astrologers and mystics were seeing it as a momentous opportunity for us to choose to manifest unconditional love on Earth.

The exquisite and powerful alignment was to be in the shape of a Star of David and was to culminate in early November 2003, the very time I had been guided to complete the 12th and final Soular Disc journey!

A few days after the call, as I opened a magazine, two short articles faced me. The first was about the 12th planet and how it had been prophesied that it would soon be rediscovered. The second was about the increasing view that the countdown to the Mayan end time of 23 December 2012 – *not* the end of the world, but a time of transformation – would commence on 23 December 2003.

This was the date I had been given to 'turn the 13th master key at Avebury'.

☷ ☀ ☷

CHAPTER 4

Alaska

CHAPTER 4

ALASKA
June 2002

During the short and exquisite summer of the far north, we had come to Alaska at the time of the June solstice to experience the grandeur of this natural sanctuary and to activate the 4th Soular Disc.

But another theme soon began to emerge for our journey. For when our group met in Anchorage, Alaska's largest settlement, we learned how bereavement had clawed at many of our lives that spring and how we had all struggled with personal losses.

Only weeks before I had left for Alaska, my dear cousin Terry had passed over after a long battle with cancer. When my dad had died when I was ten years old, it was Terry who had always been there, gentle, funny and caring. Now he was gone and I felt the dull ache of grief.

As we heard the history of the peoples of Alaska's Aleutian Islands, where we would culminate our journey to connect with the Disc, we understood that their story too was one of enormous loss.

These islands stretch in a great arc over 2,000 miles in extent from Alaska to Siberia. Here, where the arctic waters of the Bering Sea meet the warmer Pacific Ocean, are some of the most prolific fishing grounds on Earth.

For more than 9,000 years, the forefathers of today's Aleutian people enjoyed a naturally abundant life on the islands. The Aleutian islanders prospered until Russian traders arrived in the

17th century. As has been the sad case so often with meetings between so-called developed and indigenous peoples, within a few generations the ancient culture and communities of the Aleutian islanders were all but destroyed.

During World War II the remaining islanders were forced off their lands by the US military, following a brief Japanese incursion. When they were eventually allowed to return, six years later, they found their homes wrecked. And for many years thereafter it appeared that the Aleutian culture was all but dead.

*****

Our arrival in Alaska brought the answer to a question I had carried since originally receiving guidance from the Elohim about the location of the 12 Soular Discs. They had told me then that one of the Discs was centred at Mount Shasta in northern California. However, when I'd journeyed there the following year, I was surprised, disappointed and confused that energetically I hadn't felt its presence.

When I queried this with the Elohim, I was told that it had been there at the time of my original guidance but that it had completed its work there and that its energies had been shifted to Alaska.

In Anchorage we were blessed to meet Larry Merculieff, an Alutiiq elder, sacred messenger of the Hopi and healer of his people. And it was Larry who resolved the mystery of the migrating Disc!

In 1999 the Dalai Lama and other spiritual leaders had met to consider a shift in the energy of the planetary chakras from Tibet to Alaska. The shift had activated a geomantic connection running down from Alaska through the Andes of South America to support the reconciliation of the peoples of both North and South America.

Larry, as a designated peace messenger of his people, had been involved in the unfoldment of this process of collective healing.

Hearing him speak, I realized that I had sensed rightly that the energies of the Disc at Mount Shasta had indeed been transferred to Alaska in order to anchor the energies of this geomantic shift.

My friend Renae, who had journeyed to Egypt with us, had subsequently felt called to travel to Alaska, her childhood home, to work with the Soular Disc there. It was our joint guidance that had revealed that its energetic epicentre was at Akutan, a remote island in the Aleutian chain.

This location of the Alaskan Disc also continued the Discs' elemental resonance with Fire and Water. The volcanic island of Akutan, and indeed the entire Aleutian chain, forms part of the Ring of Fire, the heavily faulted geological boundary around the Pacific Ocean which marks the edge of a number of the Earth's continually moving tectonic plates.

Given that the volcano at Akutan was located on a very seismically active part of the Ring of Fire, I had a strong sense that its original location at Mount Shasta had, at least in part, ensured the latter's energetic stability over the past millennia.

I also began to understand why the journey following Alaska was to be to Peru, as activating the Soular Disc there would anchor the geomantic connection and reconciliation intuited and no doubt guided by the Dalai Lama and the other elders.

*****

Continuing to share the prophecies and wisdom of the elders of the Americas, Larry explained that they all see this as the time of a great shift and healing of human consciousness as we awake from our collective amnesia.

But the elders also foresee that as our vibrational rate increases, aspects of us that are individually and collectively out of alignment will be pushed inexorably to the surface. Emotions will intensify and for a while during the transition there will be an increase in violence on a large scale. Many people will feel profoundly restless and will be urged to radically change their lifestyles and relationships.

The Mayan elders also speak of this as a time of purification and cleansing, which will, they say, manifest in great fires – a sign to the keepers of the ancient knowledge that Mother Earth too is undergoing her own shift in awareness.

The elders speak too of an acceleration of time, which we can feel but cannot measure, as all our measuring devices are in the same frame of reference as we are ourselves. As the acceleration continues, they warn that in trying frenetically to get things done faster and faster, people will go crazy unless they pull back from the maelstrom and remain in the now of the present moment.

They unanimously ask every one of us to reconnect within ourselves and trust that our inner guidance will be there for what we need to do. They say that *we* are the ones we've been waiting for and that this is the time for our empowerment – for each of us to live our highest purpose.

These elders of the primary peoples of the Earth perceive the entire human family as embodying the four sacred colours of black, white, red and yellow. Their ancient wisdom teaches that the tribes of each colour have been gifted a particular aspect of wisdom. The red tribes embody the knowledge, understanding and nurturing of Mother Earth, the black tribes embody movement and rhythm in harmony with the Universe, the yellow tribes the mastery of breath and the white the use of energy and creativity.

Maintaining that nothing is created externally until it is embodied internally, the elders say that as the tribes of all traditions come together to share their understanding, a genetic cellular memory will awaken. They stress that this is not a return to an earlier state of consciousness, but the precursor of a collective evolutionary leap.

When we shared with Larry the intention of our journeys, he emphasized the importance of enacting spiritual prayer and ceremony on the land, whose geomantic energies are also changing and activating at this time.

He also told us that in his and many other Native American cultures, women were beginning to reassert their traditional role as healers and leaders. In this rebalancing he sees men as also shifting to their traditional role, of protecting the sacred space, so that women can do their healing work. Both men and women can then stand together, complementary and co-creative partners in the birthing of a new age.

Before we reluctantly said our farewells to Larry, he offered us one further measure of hope. For, after so long, he told us there were now the stirrings of a resurgence of the Aleutian culture and the first signs of reconciliation with the Japanese and Russian peoples. This was a great joy to him, as his own lineage was part Russian.

The focus of our service with this Soular Disc was being revealed as another pilgrimage of inner and outer healing and reconciliation.

*****

As we journeyed around the spectacular landscape of Alaska, one of the few remaining true wilderness areas on Earth, we deepened our connection with its animals and marine life and continued to hear stories of bereavement. We heard of the loss of land, culture and livelihood, some of it as recent as the catastrophic oil spill of the *Exxon Valdez* oil-tanker. We witnessed and honoured the need to grieve, knowing that this was the only way to be cleansed, to be reconciled and to move on.

I knew from personal experience that without the release of grieving, the emotional pain of personal loss could cause us to close down our hearts as a 'protection' against further pain. If we allow ourselves to grieve, however, we can let go of the trauma and enable our hearts to remain open. What we perceive as 'protection' is in fact emotional imprisonment, which can last a lifetime – or longer.

*****

Animals, plants and the wider Cosmos are all directly experienced by the native cultures of this area as conscious entities. The shaman, and indeed everyone to some degree, can communicate with and be guided by a multitude of beings, including animal and spiritual archetypes. These may include the guardian spirits of specific places in the landscape and may involve the shaman in shape-shifting.

These ancient shamanistic beliefs are currently being reawakened in the Alutiiq peoples who live in southern Alaska and the Aleutian island chain. As we journeyed through Alaska, we discovered in ways large and small that their wisdom teachings were guiding us and, to our delight, the animals, plants and elemental forces of this primeval land became our teachers.

We were now beginning to understand our human and extraterrestrial heritage at a more profound level as a result of our previous quests, and we found that this journey, which was to culminate with the activation of the Soular Disc on the solstice of 21 June 2002, took us one step further. It gave us the opportunity to re-member our intra-terrestrial heritage as ways were revealed to connect with our animal, devic and elemental brothers and sisters and to commune with Gaia.

*****

From Anchorage, as we drove north towards Denali, North America's highest mountain, the weather was typically Alaskan – grey and cloudy. Denali, 'the high one' to the Athabascan native people, stands sentinel at the apex of the mighty arc of the Alaskan mountain range. This mountain is more than twice the height of most of the other peaks in the chain, spectacularly rising over 20,000 feet above sea level. But its great height and the Alaskan weather result in many visitors never actually getting to see it.

Here in the short Alaskan summer, we enjoyed a day in the Denali National Park. The enthusiastic and knowledgeable park ranger asked us what the most important animal in the park was. Various suggestions were met with a smile and then she gave us an answer no one expected – the mosquito. The entire ecosystem relies on this tiny, and to most of us annoying, insect. It reminded us of Anita Roddick's words: 'If you think you're too small to make a difference, you've never been in bed with a mosquito.'

Stopping for a while, we got out to stretch our legs. As we idly walked and chatted, Brian suddenly hissed, 'There's a caribou.'

'No, it's a piece of wood,' I said.

'It's a caribou.'

'Are you sure?'

'Yes!'

Suddenly, the piece of wood stood up and began to lazily walk away. I followed, hardly believing the amazing sight and thrilled by the physical closeness of this majestic animal.

In the past, great herds of caribou roamed this landscape, enduring long migrations twice yearly. Both males and females grow antlers of solid bone. Shed each year during the first five years of life, as the animal grows to maturity, they are replaced by an increasingly larger set.

Shamanistic traditions pay great attention to the signs and omens of the natural world. Antlers may be seen as representing antennae, symbolizing connection to higher awareness. As our connection to the natural world around us deepened, I reflected on how the shamans read messages from the animals. I wondered if our close experience of the caribou was a signal to pay more attention to our inner perception and even perhaps a sign of its coming growth over the next few years.

*****

Arriving at the visitor centre in the heart of the park, we all gravitated to the lookout point from where the best sight of Denali – depending on the weather – was to be had. Clouds filled the sky and we accepted that we weren't going to see 'the high one' that day.

Suddenly, there was an intake of breath as someone looked up. Higher than anyone had thought possible, and perfectly centred in the only tiny patch of blue in the entire sky, was one of Denali's two peaks.

We now felt that Denali himself was welcoming us into his kingdom.

Later that day we found a quiet place in the protective shadow of the mountain and attuned to the energies of the land. Looking down at my feet, I saw a beautiful piece of green stone and gratefully accepted this as the gift of Denali. Holding it in my hand and feeling into its essence, I could sense the elemental dance of Air and Fire and clearly heard: 'This is your shield.'

As I gazed at the stone, I could see that it was indeed shaped like a shield. I then knew that from its peak high in the air to its roots deep down in the fire beneath the Earth's crust, the awesome power of Denali would always hold me safe.

And from that moment Denali's shield has been with me, physically and energetically, wherever I journey.

*****

Having experienced the majesty of Denali, we drove south. This time, the Sun shone in a cloudless sky and we felt blessed by the entire Alaskan mountain range.

Stopping to take photographs, we met an old man who had worked there for over 50 years. In all that time, he told us, he'd never known the weather better than it was today. What a precious gift Denali had bestowed on us.

We continued to appreciate the huge scale of Alaska as we drove on for hour after hour. Stopping for a while gave us the opportunity to visit one of the few remaining companies who maintain the winter use of dogs and sleds to carry people and supplies across this vast terrain. Originating with the native peoples, teams of huskies, the purest domestic descendants of wild wolves, are still used for deliveries and to conduct winter patrols in remote areas no other form of ground transport can reach.

Highly intelligent and having a strong sense of family, wolves embody much that humans aspire to. A community of wolves is hierarchical and yet the lead animal allows freedom to others in the pack – a natural balance of authority and democracy.

With their complex system of communication and subtle body language, wolves don't fight without good cause and often mate for life. With the strength and stamina to travel great distances and endure deprivation, a pack of wolves will co-operate to hunt weaker prey and so support the health of the ecosystem. And despite the old stories of the big bad wolf, there has never been a confirmed attack by a healthy wolf on a human being.

The spiritual essence of wolf medicine is deemed to embody all the above attributes and to offer psychic insight and spiritual idealism on behalf of the community.

No wonder that Native Americans revere the wolf. As I looked into the wise and gentle eyes of Duke, one of the leaders of the husky pack, I too felt that reverence.

*****

For many years I had yearned to encounter whales. Alaska is renowned for its pods of humpback whales. Reaching up to 50 feet in length and weighing up to 45 tons, these majestic beings summer here before migrating the thousands of miles to Hawaii or Mexico for the winter.

The power of whale medicine is the ancient knowledge of how to use the creative force of breath. The incredible song of the male humpback seems to embody such wisdom. Each year, the males create a new song, and to hear it is a moving reminder of an ancient memory, when we too were creatures of the seas.

Our journey took us on to the Kenai Fjords National Park at the south-eastern tip of Alaska. Here, cruise boats take visitors along the sea inlets to see at close quarters their abundance of marine life and the breathtaking sight of glaciers calving as they reach the sea after aeons of slow, slow journeying.

I was excited!

As our boat sailed into the centre of one of the fjords, the cry went up, 'There, there!'

A mother humpback whale, accompanied by her baby, probably about six months old, swam effortlessly in the middle distance. I wasn't alone in being profoundly moved by this beautiful sight, as together they cleaved the water in perfect harmony.

Almost everyone now gathered at the prow of the boat to look for more sightings, but feeling the need for some time to reflect, I walked quietly alone to the stern. My vision softened as I went into a reverie.

Suddenly and silently a huge shape rose out of the water. It was no more than 30 yards away from the boat and directly across from where I stood. Entranced, my breath caught in my chest as the ocean-grey eye of a humpback whale met mine. He – I felt it was he – poised, unmoving, his great head out of the water, while time itself was suspended.

As we silently acknowledged each other, my heart gratefully knew another miracle. Then, as unobtrusively as he had come, he sank back into the water.

Later, as I continued to feel his mighty but gentle presence, I sensed that below the threshold of my awareness he had conveyed a message for me. Sitting in my room, I saw the whale again in my inner vision. My thoughts began to dwell on the tragic discoveries of beached whales and dolphins around the world. I knew that scientists were suggesting that their electro-magnetic guidance was being scrambled and that the infra- and ultrasonic components of military communications within the oceans were causing them profound distress. And I suddenly remembered reading some years ago about a project known as HAARP, based in Alaska at a remote location called Gakoma.

HAARP is an acronym for High-frequency Active Auroral Research. Over the last few years it has been beaming pulses of extremely high-powered radio waves into the atmosphere. Ostensibly set up to improve global communications, one of its aims is to contact deep-diving nuclear submarines. Environmental groups have become increasingly concerned about the potentially catastrophic damage that such transmissions may be causing to creatures of the deep oceans such as whales, as well as to the atmosphere itself.

All of HAARP's activities are classified by the US military. The culture of paranoia and secrecy that surrounds projects such as this surely cannot be beneficial to the human collective or the greater needs of the biosphere of Gaia. Nor can the vast amounts of money spent on the military, much of it secret, be justified in a world where the basic needs within our human family are not being met.

Martin Luther King once said that we either learn to swim together or drown separately as fools. He said that each of us must make our choices in the way we perceive and live in the world. The time is surely now. There can be no more sitting on the fence or insisting 'not in my backyard' when the future of all of us depends on our swimming together.

In that moment I heard the silent plea of the whale in my heart, a poignant reminder of the truth of Martin Luther King's wisdom.

*****

Two days before the solstice, when we were to activate the 4th Soular Disc, we arrived on the tiny landing strip at Dutch Harbour Unalaska, our base in the Aleutian Islands. From here we had planned to fly by seaplane to Akutan, where the energies of the Disc are centred.

On entering the arrivals hall, I heard my name being called, only to be given the disappointing news that the seaplane needed repairs and there was no chance of it being airworthy for our onward flight.

After the respite of the last few days, when the theme of letting go, grieving and reconciliation had seemed to recede, it now resumed its central presence in our ongoing journey. We collectively let go of any expectations and allowed ourselves to be in the flow of whatever understanding and healing were to come.

Renae's local knowledge, however, was about to save the day. During her earlier journey here to make arrangements for our group, she'd met the skipper of a boat who she felt might be able to take us to Akutan.

Unlike the seaplane, the journey by boat in what could be rough conditions would make it a very long day. But everyone was in agreement. If the skipper and his boat were available, this is what we would do. If not, we all accepted that we would be wherever we were meant to be to activate the Soular Disc.

Renae went off to meet the skipper and soon returned with the good news that yes, he would take us.

*****

Early on the clear bright morning of 21 June we arrived at the boatyard in good time. As we made our way to our own boat, I noticed the name of another moored there: *Miss Terry*. I cried a smile at this reminder of my dear Terry and the truth of how much I missed him.

Looking up, we saw high above us three golden eagles soaring effortlessly, forming a perfect triangle in the cloudless sky, the symbolism of their trinity speaking to us of reconciliation and resolution.

To Native Americans, the golden eagle is an embodiment of the spirit of the Sun. There is a legend that as an eagle ages it will fly ever higher towards the Sun, almost burning itself up in doing so. It will then seek a source of pure water and, swooping down, dip its wings three times, restoring its youth and reconciling the energies of Fire and Water.

The golden trinity of eagles and their mythic connection with the elemental essences embodied by the Soular Discs gifted us yet another wonderful omen. We knew that the spirits of the animals were speaking to us and that our connection would be all that it was meant and needed to be.

After a long and bumpy sea crossing, during which some of us, me included, turned the same colour as the ocean that buoyed us on, we gratefully landed at Akutan's tiny and only jetty. Here we were met by Renae's Aleutian friends, who would join us on the boat ride to the far side of the island.

Seasonal workers who come to process the fish caught in these abundant waters swell the population of this small island. Renae's friends were some of the very few people who live here the whole year round; indeed, two of them had never left the tiny island. They understood our spiritual purpose for being here and their support and comradeship were a joyful blessing to us.

*****

The skipper skilfully steered the boat through the increasingly choppy coastal waters to a small inlet leading to a hidden valley of hot springs where Renae and I had both felt the Disc's energies to be their most powerful.

In the cramped space of the boat we helped each other to don our bulky life jackets. Excitedly, we readied ourselves to enter the small landing craft for the final part of our long journey to connect with the Disc.

But in those last few moments, looking at the surf pounding the steep and rocky beach that would be our only place to land, the skipper realized the sea was too rough for us to safely land and then return.

As he and Renae told me of our situation, I knew I had to make an immediate choice that would decide the outcome of all we had undergone together. I could argue and rail against his judgement, resentful and frustrated that now, of all days, and having come so far, we were halted on the final threshold of our cherished destination. Or I could let go of my plan and release myself and the others, trusting that all was well and that we were where we needed to be.

I chose to let go.

As, with the most beautiful grace, did everyone else.

Quietly we formed a circle in the small space on the deck of the boat, steadying ourselves as it rocked in the heavy swell. What few words came, of intention, dedication and blessing, were quickly dispersed on the wind and only what we felt deep within remained with us.

As we joined hands with our Aleutian friends and connected with the Soular Disc, its gentle energies were a balm for our souls. Against the backdrop of sea, wind and crashing waves, we silently offered prayers for the letting go of old pain, for the release of grief and for ultimate reconciliation.

The simplicity of this moment belied all the complexity that had brought us to this place at this time. As I stood buffeted by the wind swirling around us, I thought of all the torturous ways in which we continue to replay old hurts and find new ways of adding to them. And I realized that however deep those hurts and however justifiable our pain, the choice is ultimately simple: hold on or let go. To remain imprisoned by the past or to be free for the future.

Suddenly, bright golden light suffused my inner vision and I smiled as I realized that the Disc was activated.

To complete our work here, I took out the stone I had carried from Rawak in China and offered it with gratitude to the Aleutian goddess and guardian of the sea, Sedna.

Later, at the small jetty, saying our farewells to our Aleutian friends, I asked and received permission to take a small pebble from the beach there, an energetic rainbow bridge to the next Disc in Peru.

Some time afterwards, we discovered that the following week a representation of the Japanese people was to come to the island. The following year, a representation of the Russian people also planned to come, along with others from all the Aleutian peoples who had been disenfranchised over the years.

Reconciliation had begun.

*****

After a brief rest we'd intended to fly back to Anchorage and then home. What we hadn't realized was that at this time of year the unsettled weather could prevent planes from landing at Dutch Harbour and we were now warned that we could be delayed for a week or more. Given that I had a very important personal reason for wanting to get home – my fiancé Tony and I were about to be married – it was yet another lesson in letting go!

The delay of our scheduled flight – which eventually happened three times – also guided us to realize that there was something else we needed to do here. For some, it offered time for reflection and space to undergo an inner reconciliation. For others, it gifted a further opportunity to pray for the reconciliation of this incredible land and its peoples.

For all of us, the wonderful abundance of eagles on Unalaska was an ever-present joy, even though to the locals the eagles were sometimes a 'darned nuisance'. Despite hoping to find discarded feathers, though, none of us did. But just before we left, ignorant of the prohibition against taking such feathers unless we were Native Americans, some of us were gifted feathers by a local man. He gave me a beautiful feather, which I planned to take home for Tony.

Walking along the deserted beach at Dutch Harbour during the last moments before leaving for our fourth, and successful, attempt to fly home, I was guided to pick up a few blue-grey pebbles as a reminder of our journey. Meandering further along the beach than I'd intended, I had decided to turn back when I clearly heard 'Three more pebbles' and so walked on. I picked up the first, then, a few yards further on, the second. As I stooped to pick up the third and final pebble, a little way beyond it I saw the most exquisite eagle feather lying directly across my path.

As we made ready to return home, I offered a prayer of gratitude to all the beings in all the realms of the Aleutian cosmos who had guided and protected us.

'*Quyanásinaq,*' I said in the Aleutian tongue. 'Thank you.'

*****

Days after I returned from Alaska, my beloved Tony and I were married and I took his surname of Currivan, a Celtic name meaning 'raven'.

To the Druids, the geomancers of the ancient Celts, the raven was a sacred bird of protection, especially on the field of battle. As a carrion bird, it was also seen as a bird of death, able to carry messages between the worlds. Its ability to fly to the darkest regions of the underworld and there to retrieve oracular knowledge made it the companion and guide of shamanic healers.

When I'd arrived in Alaska, I had also become aware of Raven's spiritual significance to the tribes of the Pacific northwest. They teach that Raven brought light and order to the world by stealing sunlight from one who would keep the world in darkness. Nothing could exist without Raven, and in him, human and animal spirits intermingle. Raven channels the creative life-force used to work the magic of spiritual laws upon the Earth plane. He is the messenger of change and transformation.

Raven medicine embodies all this and it was an honour to take on this resonance in Tony's name.

Ten days later we left for the 5th Soular Disc journey, to Peru, together with 24 fellow travellers – it was clearly not to be a quiet honeymoon!

As we prepared to gather in Cusco, the centre of the ancient Incan Empire, I again remembered that His Holiness the Dalai Lama had spoken of the new consciousness being activated in Alaska and connecting the energies of North and South America.

Tony and I asked for a blessing on whatever part we were to play in this rainbow bridge of awakening.

❄ ❄ ❄

CHAPTER 5

Peru

CHAPTER 5

PERU

July 2002

Returning to Peru felt wonderful and I eagerly anticipated the journey ahead. My connection with the devic realms of Pacha Mama, as the Peruvian priests call the living Earth, and the *apukuna*, the great mountain spirits, was joyful and becoming ever more profound. And once again I looked forward to John, Bonita and Jorge arranging an unforgettable experience for everyone.

Some months earlier, I'd shared with John and Bonita my guidance that the timing of our coming journey was important and that it should coincide with the festival of Qoyllur R'iti. John and I were only aware of the Qoyllur R'iti that took place at the June solstice. This was confusing, because the Elohim had also guided that we should be in Alaska at that time. John was also concerned by the thought of the huge crowds that would attend the solsticial festival.

Thankfully, Bonita was able to resolve the confusion when she told us that there were in fact two festivals of the same name, the second one celebrating the birth of the Incan New Year at the end of July. This was the Qoyllur R'iti my guidance had referred to.

The words of the Dalai Lama now shed further light on the timing of our being in Alaska at the solstice – the time of the first Qoyllur R'iti – and in Peru at the time of the second, birthing the geomantic connection between the Americas at this cosmically synchronous moment.

*****

Our large group, some of whom had joined us on previous Soular Disc quests, began our journey in the Incan capital Cusco, which in the native Quechua language is Qosqo, 'the navel of the world'. It was here in the Temple of Corocancha, the House of the Sun, that 17th-century chronicler Garcilaso de la Vega had said 'a golden disc' was safeguarded.

The walls of the Corocancha were literally covered in gold. De la Vega's account of the physical form of the Disc was that it too was made of gold and was so large that it took up the entire forward part of the Temple.

Its energies may well have formed the nexus of the Incan spiritual power. Some 40 rays of telluric energies, or *ceques,* both physically and energetically radiated from the Corocancha to all directions of the Incan Empire. A variety of shrines and sacred sites were constructed along their paths, built on vortices of both inward and outward energy flows and thus continually reinvigorating the empire of these sons of the Sun.

Finding a quiet place within the temple, we stood silently together, attuning ourselves to the energies of the Soular Disc. Only sensing its presence as a faint echo, I felt that it had indeed been here before the cataclysmic arrival of the Spaniards, when it had been secreted for safekeeping in the depths of Lake Titicaca.

*****

While based at Cusco, we explored its spectacular Incan ruins.

The Andean cosmos comprises three worlds, all of which are imbued with *kawsay,* or life-force. The metaphysical upper and lower worlds lie above and below the Earth plane and each is archetypally embodied by a power animal – the lower world by the serpent, the Earth plane by the puma or jaguar and the upper world by the condor.

The layout of Cusco forms a geomythic puma and its energetic environs form a microcosm of the entire Earth plane. Above the city, the great ruins of Sacsayhuaman depict the head of the puma, whose vast jaws form ramparts around an amphitheatre open to the sky. These massive walls of stone zigzag for some 2,000 feet, forming three tiers of megalithic engineering. Exquisitely shaped in three dimensions, they create a precise interlocking pattern of massive stones, one weighing a gigantic 300 tons.

Entering Sacsayhuaman, we came upon a wall-bounded field of natural boulders, each representing one of the *apukuna*, the great spirits of the surrounding mountains. These were offering their benevolent guardianship into this sacred place.

Vivid memories of my earlier experience of Peru and of the presence of the *apukuna* nearly three years before returned to me. Then I had felt like a very young and inexperienced apprentice ready to learn their age-old Earth wisdom.

I sensed Denali's presence here too, as though introducing me to his kin.

The essence of these great spirits of the mountains felt huge and yet intimate, familiar yet unknowable. Crowned by the sky and rooted deep in the Earth, the energy of each resonates with all four elements. As I asked for their blessing on our journey I sensed, with a smile of gratitude, that they were willing to teach me more.

*****

We were now to journey in the midst of the Peruvian Andes, along the Sacred Valley of the Incas, which stretches for more than 60 miles from Pisaq to the mysterious hidden city of Machu Picchu. For millennia, the valley and its revered river Vilcanota have been associated with the Mayu, the celestial river of the Milky Way, which serves as a cosmic and ritual axis for the Andean peoples.

In the centre of the valley lies the temple complex of Ollantytambo, one of my favourite places in Peru. At its entrance we cleansed ourselves in stone basins filled with the snow-cold water that cascades down from the surrounding mountains. Then, slowly climbing a steep staircase of stone surrounded by terraces cut into the natural slope, we came to the entrance to the unfinished Temple of the Sun.

Pausing to regain our breath in this high altitude, we turned and gazed across the valley to the mountain of Pinkuylluna, where we could make out an enormous and powerful sculpted image of the Incan creator god Wiracocha, 150 feet in height. Here, at the December solstice, the first rays of the Sun illuminate the crown of Wiracocha, in effect reawakening, with each yearly cycle, his and our higher consciousness.

The Temple of Ollantaytambo, as so many other sacred sites around the world, intentionally incorporates acoustic effects. These were not silent monuments. The ancients understood the nature of sound and how to work with its powerful resonance, to heal or destroy.

As at the great majority of such places of ancient resonance, here it is the lower male tones that embody the greatest effects. So, facing one of the square niches cut into the wall that overlooks the grail of the valley below, I chanted as deeply as I could. The sonic reverberation engulfed me as I experienced just a tiny proportion of the power that would have been generated here by a priesthood trained for such work.

*****

In our exploration of the temple, we all eventually found our way to a wall of six huge blocks of red stone. From my previous visit I knew that archaeologists had determined that the nearest source of this stone was many miles away down the mountain, across the valley and over the mountain at its other side. How the ancients transported the six massive blocks to the temple remains a mystery. Was it by superhuman effort or did they, as so many legends around the world maintain, use acoustic resonance to levitate them into place?

During that earlier visit, our group meditation had revealed that the red stones resonated energetically with human consciousness. It seems that the iron with which they are suffused and which gives them their red colour attunes to the vibration of human consciousness as embodied in the iron-rich haemoglobin of our blood. Dependent on the awareness level of the human beings journeying here, the stones act as a conduit to higher consciousness.

Higher up in the ruins of the temple is a quiet room now open to the sky and rarely visited. Here during that earlier visit and again now, as we meditated, a number of us experienced a profound connection with extraterrestrial beings from the Pleiades.

On each of the two visits, synchronous meetings with local mystics, who are the contemporary priests of this sacred place, gently validated our understanding and experiences of the Pleiadians, who are now communicating directly with ever more people as we individually and collectively expand our awareness and re-member our hidden history and future destiny as cosmic beings.

*****

Our home during Qoyllur R'iti was near Pisaq in the Sacred Valley, where Carol Cumes has created a healing sanctuary called Willka T'ika. It was a joy to see Carol again and feel the nurturing energies of her sanctuary, whose name means 'Sacred flower' in the Quechua language.

Carol's garden is overlooked and guarded by an ancient Lucma tree and, intuitively guided, she has laid out the garden geomantically and filled it with organically grown vegetables and healing herbs. The venerable Don Martín Quispi, a Q'ero elder and priest, trekked from his home high on the sacred mountain of Ausangate to lead us here in ceremony in celebration and blessing of the New Year.

The few remaining Q'ero people are the direct descendants of the Incas and are seen as the custodians of their highest wisdom. Living high up on Ausangate, they were never discovered by the Spanish and remained safe in their isolation until the early 1990s.

Through a long life of healing service Don Martín has been revered for his ability to work with the unseen worlds and especially to commune with the *apukuna*. This tiny nut-brown man exuded profound and gentle spiritual authority. We all sat together in the beautiful garden of Willka T'ika while on everyone's behalf he made an offering to Pacha Mama and Papa Inti, Mother Earth and Father Sun, to celebrate the coming year and ask for blessings.

Carefully laying out an altar, Don Martín constructed a complex *despacho,* or offering, made up of tiny representations of all aspects of life and the Cosmos, from flowers and seeds to tiny plastic replicas of items in everyday life. Each was dedicated by the offering of a *kuka k'intu* of coca leaves.

The Andean peoples use coca leaves on all sacred occasions, and excavations of ancient pre-Incan burial sites have shown that they were also used ceremoniously many thousands of years ago. The ritual of *kuka k'intu* involves choosing three unblemished leaves, which are held together in the hand and then raised to the lips. A silent prayer calling on Pacha Mama and the spirits of the mountains is then made, as the breath is blown through the leaves three times. Then they are released.

Each of us added our own prayers in a *kuka k'intu* before Don Martín made a bundle of the entire *despacho.* Slowly walking around the circle we had formed, he blessed each of us with the concentrated power of the *despacho.* With final prayers, he then burned the offering to release and empower its sacred intention of bringing abundance, peace and joy in the coming year.

*****

While at Willka T'ika, surrounded by the abundance of elemental energies, I led the group in a guided meditation, which to my surprise and gratitude the spirit of the mountain here had spontaneously given to me during my first visit, three years before. It was:

> In your inner vision, as you gaze around, you are standing in a lush and fragrant valley. Your eyes are drawn to its far end, where the flanks of a high snow-covered mountain rise majestically up and up. As your gaze follows, you feel yourself becoming lighter and find yourself high up at the snow-line of the mountain.
>
> You can hear the trickle of a tiny stream, birthed from the melting snow. As you move towards it, you feel yourself begin to melt and become one with the water.
>
> Flowing down the mountainside, you begin to gather snow-fed water from other streams, growing larger and flowing faster. Over and around rocks you tumble, bubbling with life.
>
> You begin to sense tiny fish swimming within you and plants reaching towards the Sun through your nurturing depths.
>
> As you leap over waterfalls and rush through rapids, you become larger and larger. On reaching the valley you have grown into a river.
>
> Moving more slowly, you wend a sinuous path along the valley and then out into the open plain.

You now begin to feel the call of the distant ocean, as if from an ancient memory, and flow towards its embrace.

The freshness of your water reaches into the salty currents as you begin to feel the pulse of the tides.

Diving deep and deeper still, you explore your new domain.

Playing with dolphins, singing the songs of the whales and dancing in the foam of the waves, you luxuriate in the richness of the sea, the birthing-place of all life on Earth.

You feel now the ebb and flow of tides within you and begin to feel the inexorable pull of the white goddess of the Moon shining in the sky above.

As you are drawn towards the distant shore, you see a sea cliff rising majestically above the water, at its base a dark womb-like cave, worn over millennia by the pounding waves.

You are called into the cave, each wave carrying you closer and closer.

You rush deep into the cave and spray your energy into the glistening rock.

And become the rock.

You begin to delve deep into this new world.

Exploring caves of shining crystal, millions of years in the growing, you learn the ancient secrets of the living Earth. You are entranced by diamond, quartz, amethyst and sapphire, each with their own vibration and story.

You sense warmth seeping through you as you journey

ever deeper and enter the liquid realms of magma and, through their own eternal tides, reach the crystal heart of the Earth.

Here you can feel the heartbeat of Gaia and, nurtured by her, know that you are her beloved child.

Rising once more through the magma and rock, you taste the richness of the life-sustaining soil and sense its many creatures before standing on the high cliff overlooking the ocean.

You now feel the Sun's warmth and look up into the bright blue of the sky.

A small white cloud seems to playfully beckon you and you find yourself floating, becoming lighter and lighter.

You have become the very essence of air – the clouds, the wind and the thunder. Now a gentle breeze and now a hurricane, you may roam where you will, high above the Earth.

You feel yourself become part and then all of the great weather cycles that nurture all the creatures of Gaia, through all the seasons of all the years, ever the same and ever changing.

You pause, breathing deeply of the clear air, and see in the distance the huge shape of a mountain and float towards its snow-capped summit.

As you approach, you peer down and notice a small campfire shining brightly, just below the snow-line. Its crackling energy calls you and as you move towards it, you feel yourself becoming its warmth.

As you bathe in the flames at its heart, you feel yourself expand as its fiery energy flows through you.

You glow brightly, inspired and alive with creativity.

Looking out, you see a seated shaman, wise and powerful, looking deep into the flames.

Looking more closely, you see that the face of the shaman is your own reflection.

You are the wise one.

Emerging from the fire, you become the wholeness of your human self – Water, Earth, Air and Fire, the elemental you, the human embodiment of Gaia.

Leaving the fire to be cooled by the night air, you begin to walk down the mountain, intimately knowing each step of the way home.

Afterwards, when we shared our experiences of this meditation, I discovered yet again how powerful this inner connection with the elemental realms could be, and thanked the spirit of the mountain for his inspiration.

*****

The night before we left Willka T'ika, I had a strange dream. Sharing its details with the others the following morning, I realized that it had involved Geronimo, the great peacekeeper of the North American native tribes. I sensed that his presence had something to do with bringing together the eagle and the condor, the two great symbols of North and South American spirituality.

We had connected with the eagle in Alaska – would the energy of the condor guide us here?

The following day, before journeying on, we couldn't resist a visit to the vibrant market of Pisaq. As we wandered around the stalls, a number of us felt drawn to a tiny shop offering artefacts and crafts. On the back wall was a poster of Geronimo.

I felt that this was a further sign that we were on track – in service to the activation of the geomantic bridge between North and South America, anchored by the Soular Discs in Alaska and Peru, and given wings by the eagle and the condor.

*****

The first sight of the enigmatic ruins of Machu Picchu is always breathtaking. Exquisitely beautiful, they generously welcome those who respect the ancient ways.

The Spanish conquistadors never discovered this Incan sanctuary. Its white granite temples and dwellings are built on a limestone plateau cradled between the summits of the mountains Machu Picchu and Huayna Picchu, way above the Vilcanota river.

The three Andean worlds of the serpent, the jaguar and the condor energetically and physically meet here. The river Vilcanota sinuously flowing around Machu Picchu in the valley far below is the embodiment of the archetypal serpent. High above, the shape of Huayna Picchu represents the magnificent condor of the upper world. And on the top level of the ruins is a massive stone, known as 'the funerary rock'. Here, if you are ready, you may meet the essence of the jaguar.

During my first visit to Machu Picchu, three years before, we had been granted permission to remain in the ruins after they had closed for the night and the many other visitors had left. On that occasion, climbing high up above the ruins, we had come in silence to the funerary rock.

In many traditions, each initiation into a more profound awareness of the Cosmos engenders the metaphorical death of our old self and a rebirth into the new being we have become. Here, each of us was to lie on the rock and undergo the initiation of the death and rebirth ceremony.

One by one we had walked forward to the rock, helped and supported by our companions. When it was my turn, I lay down, committing myself to an emptying of the past and the willingness to embrace an unknown future.

As I closed my eyes, I could see in my inner vision a great jaguar. Carrying me on its back, it leaped up into the sky. I felt us fly together in a huge arc through the heavens and, looking down, could see my physical body still lying on the funerary rock, a tiny speck far below. Simultaneously, I could also sense myself in my physical body looking up at my flight with the jaguar.

As I could feel my aetheric being flying back down to merge once more with my physical being, I couldn't resist opening my eyes. Gazing up at the beautiful full orb of the Moon above me, I saw the jaguar emerge and in that moment I felt reborn.

*****

On this visit, we again had the opportunity to undergo the initiation of the death and rebirth ceremony. A few chose not to, however, and this time I elected to remain with them. We made our way to the principal temple of Machu Picchu, where one by one we approached the altar and offered ourselves to the higher purpose of our journey.

Then, together, we continued on to the Temple of the Condor, which is shaped to mirror this sacred being of the upper world. On its floor is the sculpted outline of the head of the condor and lying here many people have experienced visions.

Forming a circle around its head, we each in turn lay prostrate on the condor, facing the ground. With our arms spread wide, we 'flew' on the condor's back to inner revelation.

Sharing our experiences afterwards, we found that a number of us had sensed a powerful extraterrestrial presence and when I had been lying on the condor one of the group had, in their inner vision, seen lights dance around and through my body and enter the rock of the temple across from my head.

Then another person revealed that they had seen the same thing. The only difference was that their eyes had been open – a confirmation that, as the journeys to come would continue to teach us, the veils between the inner and outer worlds were becoming ever thinner.

*****

The next day we returned to Machu Picchu and to the lower levels of the city, where a rock thrusts out from the side of the cliff. Angled to enable a person to lie on it with their feet to the cliff-face and their head out over the valley below, this 'flying rock' offers an exercise in trust and letting go.

Clambering one by one onto the rock, we each chose to 'fly' lying on our back, our arms outstretched to the Sun. It is said that if the protection of the *apukuna* is requested, this opportunity to 'fly' is sacred and safe. Nevertheless, Bonita and I held – or offered to hold – everyone by their legs or feet, depending on their own sense of adventure and trust in the spirits of the mountains!

After everyone had braved the flying rock, they slowly wandered off to spend some time individually exploring Machu Picchu. As I was about to leave, I heard, uncomfortably clearly, 'Fly from the rock.'

Aware that I was being asked to stand upright on the small edge of the rock rather than lie along its length, I wasn't sure if I had the courage to comply. But the four *apukuna* of the mountains that surround the city are awesome presences and I knew that it was they, Machu Picchu, Huayna Picchu, Putucusi and Yanantin, who were asking this of me.

I inched out along the rock and finally stood on its end.

Breathing deeply to calm my fear, I knew the four *apukuna* were safeguarding me as I looked far out across the valley and slowly raised my arms high, as though in flight. Closing my eyes,

I could see myself as the condor, wheeling above the mountain peaks and at one with them.

Inching back along the length of the flying rock, I felt elated and incredibly grateful for this initiation into the element of Air.

Later, a few of us climbed the dizzying heights of Huayna Picchu, overlooking the city. Gazing down thousands of feet, we saw Machu Picchu lying exquisitely below us, its sacred precincts and terraces forming the shape of a hummingbird.

The hummingbird is sacred to native peoples throughout the Americas and they celebrate it as embodying tireless joy and the ability to drink deep of the sweet nectar of life.

This beautiful shape of the city, expressed in the pure white of its buildings set against the verdant green of its landscape, is poignantly only able to be perceived from this height. In the sunshine of a glorious day, we too drank deep of its sweet presence.

An inclined rock which forms the summit of Huayna Picchu offers the highest of vantage points. Climbing to its very edge, I looked outwards and again felt the power of the condor rise up within me. I knew then that the promise of the rainbow bridge between the eagle and the condor had been fulfilled, and I thanked each of the *apukuna* for their priceless gift.

*****

Leaving Machu Picchu, we returned to the lower reaches of the Sacred Valley. Thanks to Bonita and Jorge, we were now honoured by the invitation of a local healer to visit his recent rediscovery, which he called the Pacha Mama Temple.

High up a precipitous but climbable cliff, the temple was constructed within a high-domed cave. As we helped each other to climb up to it, I looked and saw three faces naturally formed in the contours of the cliffs. These guardians of the temple appeared to be beckoning us on.

At the entrance to the temple was a great stone altar in the form of the Andean cross, or *chicana,* that represents the three worlds of their cosmos. As each of us in turn stepped up to the altar, the healer, speaking sacred words of blessing and release, cleansed us with a great condor feather.

The energies here were profoundly moving and as we all held the space for the one who was being blessed, I felt great sobs well up within me. In this ancient place I was overwhelmed by a deep reverence for Pacha Mama and how over the aeons she has nurtured all her children.

Eventually it was my turn, and as I dedicated myself in continuing service to Spirit, I could feel the presence of three beings around me – the guardians who had earlier welcomed us here. I did not share this experience with the others, but later one of the group told me that he had clearly seen three smiling Incan priests around me.

*****

The Incas measured time in great cosmic cycles, called Suns, each lasting 1,000 years. These cyclic waves were perceived as being made up of a 500-year period of light followed by 500 years of darkness.

At the completion of the last period of light, five centuries ago, the Spanish arrived. Light-skinned and arriving from the sea, the way the legendary Wiracocha, the great white creator god, had been prophesied to return, they were welcomed – and went on to destroy the Incan Empire.

Now, after 500 years of ensuing darkness, the Incan cycles presage a return of the light. Over the last decade, the Q'eros, the spiritual messengers of the people, have revealed a number of prophecies for this time. These include the coming identification, at the Temple of Wiracocha at Raqchi, of two new Incas, one man and one woman, who will be chosen from a group of 12 initiates from all traditions and cultures around the world. The prophecy says that they will be recognized by their shining appearance, like the Incas of old, who were reputed to shine with the radiance of the Sun. In turn, it is said, they will herald the rediscovery of the long-lost sacred city of Paititi, whose wisdom will then be available to the world once more.

The next day a long drive lay ahead of us over the Alto Plano, the incredibly dry high plateau of Peru's hinterland, to Lake Titicaca. On our way was Raqchi. Remembering the Q'eros' prophecy of the coming Incas, we wondered what we might discover there.

During the journey, I recalled the legends of Wiracocha. When he arrived at Raqchi, in his form of a tall white man, it is said that the Indians didn't recognize him and rushed violently towards him. Seeing their aggression, Wiracocha caused a great volcanic eruption, with fire falling down from the sky. Realizing his power, the Indians fell to their knees before him. Wiracocha then hit the ground with his staff, causing the volcano to cease erupting forever.

In gratitude, the Indians of Raqchi created a splendid temple where Wiracocha caused the eruption to halt, and housed a man-sized statue of him within it. When the Spaniards arrived, they tore down this temple and plundered the statue of Wiracocha, taking it to Cusco, where it too was eventually destroyed. Incredibly, however, parts of it were later rediscovered. The head was taken to Spain, where it still remains, and the chest was found in 1950 when the local tourist office was being rebuilt after a great earthquake that destroyed much of Cusco.

Raqchi seems to be waiting for something whose time has not yet come. Could it be that to fulfil the Q'ero prophecy the remains of Wiracocha must be returned to Raqchi? Perhaps only time will tell.

*****

As we drew closer to Lake Titicaca we encountered the gargantuan stone towers at Sillustani. On a small peninsula near Lake Titicaca, they overlook the smaller Lake Umayo, from whose waters a central island emerges. The pure and peaceful lake reflects the sky so perfectly that the island appears to be floating on the clouds. Jorge told us of the legends associating UFOs with the island and the lake, and the energies here are powerful and indeed otherworldly.

At other sacred sites around the world, there are many instances of circular towers being built ostensibly as burial places or for defence. Yet geomancers have long understood that their primary purpose was to balance energies and in many cases, to enhance the fertility of the surrounding land.

At Sillustani there are also two ancient stone circles that Jorge referred to as 'the circles of the Sun and Moon'. As we walked each in turn and dowsed their energies, it was clear that they both embodied spiral vortices. Our consensus was that the energies of the Sun circle radiated outwards, whereas the spiral vortex of the Moon circle was inward.

Together, these two formed a perfect balance connecting the Earth and the greater Cosmos, embodying the cosmic principles of yin and yang. And as we walked our own spirals within them, we felt that connection and the empowerment of that balance deep within ourselves.

*****

Arriving at Jorge's comfortable hotel near the shore of Lake Titicaca, our home for the culmination of our journey, we readied ourselves for our connections with the portal of Amaru Muru and then with the Soular Disc.

Since my last visit to the portal, located inland from the lake, it had come to be called 'the Peruvian star-gate'.

As we approached the base of a massive red cliff along which runs a waist-high low stone platform, I gazed at the portal that I'd so often recalled in my inner vision since my first visit. Located at the centre of the platform and carved into the cliff-face, it is shaped like a small door. The natural cliff above is in the unmistakable shape of a reclining woman. At either end of the platform and running vertically up the cliff are two channels, which reach up to her body of stone. Jorge and Bonita explained how the energy spiralled up the channel to the right of the door and then down the other channel.

We arranged ourselves in a semi-circle facing the cliff-face portal, supporting in turn each person's experience of the two peripheral vertical channels and the central portal. When it was my turn, as I knelt and placed my forehead on the door, I immediately passed through it and energetically entered an incredibly bright landscape. In my inner vision I recognized what Jorge calls the Temple of Illumination. Energetically experiencing the temple as a circular building open to the Cosmos, I could see that instead of walls it was surrounded by 12 luminescent columns that I recognized as embodying the multi-dimensional energies of the Soular Discs.

As I entered the temple, I felt enormous energies flow through me, as though I was at the centre of a vast matrix of consciousness, and I could hear the Elohim explain that awareness of our individual and collective human, extraterrestrial and intraterrestrial heritage could be accessed from here. I knew too that from this moment I would be able to return energetically to the temple and bring others here for their own illumination.

Rejoining my companions, I resumed my energetic place in supporting the others to experience their own truths.

Suddenly I felt very faint. Needing to sit down before I fell, I found myself facing the portal. Looking up at the reclining stone figure above the cliff, I now saw that one of the two vertical channels reached up to the alter-major chakra at the back of the figure's head and the other reached her solar plexus chakra. I saw too that the portal itself rested below her heart chakra.

I could now feel energy flowing between the heart, mind and will of the figure and realized that this Peruvian star-gate was a portal of the 8th chakra of the universal heart. It had been my vulnerability that had enabled me to see.

Before leaving, I climbed up to the reclining figure and there, high above the portal, chose a small pebble to carry on as the rainbow bridge to the next Soular Disc in Australia.

Sitting there quietly alone, I could also feel the powerful energies of the Disc radiating from the depths of Lake Titicaca calling us to complete our work in Peru.

*****

The Uros people of Lake Titicaca live on floating islands constructed of reeds. It was during a meditation on such an island during my first visit that my initial connection to the Soular Disc had broken my heart open and begun the process of re-membering that had led me back here now.

Once again we journeyed by boat out to one of the reed villages. After being welcomed by the villagers, we settled ourselves in a circle to connect with the Disc. This time, our work was to activate its connection as part of the global unity grid anchored by all 12 Soular Discs.

Looking around our circle, I could sense the long, long journeys that everyone had made to be together at this moment, in this place. Each person was here to play their unique role, and did so immaculately.

Simply and quietly, we energetically opened our hearts to act as conduits for the unconditionally loving energies of the Disc. And each of us, in our own way, pledged ourselves to heal into the wholeness of who we really are, in service to the greater embodiment of Heaven on Earth. At the culmination of our connection, we passed to each other the pebble from Akutan, each adding our healing intention. Then Jorge and I slowly walked to the edge of the floating island and offered the pebble to the deep waters of the lake.

Afterwards, we mingled with the villagers and bought some of their home-made crafts – a practical way of thanking these lovely people for their hospitality and sensitivity to our purpose.

One old lady sat quietly in the background. She spoke no English, but as a number of us approached her and smiled, we all felt her powerfully loving energy. She had been all but invisible and we never discovered who she was, yet we knew that it was her presence that had blessed our connection with the Disc.

*****

The profound insights that came forward in Peru were in stark contrast to my experiences as part of the group. Arriving home feeling deeply vulnerable and emotionally drained, I realized that my feelings were more than natural tiredness after a long journey. I was so depleted and dispirited that, with only five of the Soular Disc connections completed, I wasn't sure I had the inner resources to go on.

As I looked back on the journey, I began to understand that my feelings had arisen from a sense of being 'invisible' within the group. Almost from the moment of our arrival I'd been aware of energetic undercurrents in the group, and as time had gone on, I'd felt more and more unheard and excluded.

Despite my repeated requests, the itinerary that had been arranged had left little time to explore the stated purpose of our journey. Instead, the shamanic content had been repeatedly emphasized and the deeper understanding of the Soular Discs and their wider context marginalized. I had felt increasingly power-less and humiliated, and had eventually withdrawn from attempts to influence the unfolding situation.

Now, as I reflected, I became aware that the universal heart connection with the Discs asked something of us in return – a willingness to undergo a profound and emotional inner journey of healing by facing our deepest emotional fears and embracing them.

It was only now that I began to appreciate the incredible gift that everyone who had journeyed to Peru had offered me.

When I spoke to some of the others, we realized that receiving profound insights through the vulnerability of feeling invisible had been a recurring theme for a number of us. Emma, one of our fellow travellers who had also journeyed to Egypt and China with us, shared her feelings, which were similar to my own, and offered the insight that the legend of the Peruvian Disc reflected our own experiences. Its journey too had required it to be both visible, at the Corocancha in Cusco, and then invisible, as it returned to Lake Titicaca to await its time to re-emerge.

Realizing that I'd felt the responsibility for the journeys as a personal mission – and indeed burden – I knew that to continue I must somehow transcend my ego desire for recognition. As I remembered the silent and almost invisible old lady on the reed island at Lake Titicaca, I understood that my work with the Soular Discs was asking me to be both visible and invisible – to embody both visible empowerment and to be in invisible service to the greater power of love.

While our mind does a wonderful job of perceiving our individuality, our connection to the wholeness of the Cosmos is ultimately through the heart. And by living in the energy of the universal heart, I would find the way home.

I finally understood!

I was beginning to appreciate too that the insights that were continuing to unfold throughout the journeys did so in a way that was often unplanned and always unexpected. I recognized that in order to be open to more profound depths of healing, we had to be willing to be ever more co-creative with others and to allow our spontaneity to open the portal to miracles.

The coming journeys were to offer unfolding opportunities for every one of us to let go and trust – but the validation arising from our willingness to do so would be returned beyond measure, time and time again.

Peru, however, was to be the last Soular Disc journey which John Buzenberg would arrange. From now on – with John's blessing – it felt appropriate for us to co-organize the journeys ourselves. And it seemed that in no time at all we were preparing for our November departure to Australia.

☷ �☀ ☷

CHAPTER 6

Australia

AUSTRALIA

November 2002

In November of 2002 our small group met in Australia for a combined journey there and then on to New Zealand to activate the 6th and 7th Discs.

In Australia we would begin our journey in Sydney and then fly inland to the Red Heart. This vast expanse of red desert makes up one of the oldest landforms on Earth and there we were to connect geomantically with the great natural monolith of Uluru, or Ayer's Rock, and the even larger Kata Tjuta, where, the Elohim had guided me, the epicentre of the energies of the 6th Soular Disc was located.

We were also to spend a few days far out in the bush with an Aboriginal family – a rare privilege and one to which we were very much looking forward.

*****

Craig Cotterill has lived in the bush all his life. His father, Jim, too. When Jim was growing up, he played with an Aboriginal boy about the same age. And now Jim, Craig and Craig's baby daughter have a three-generational relationship with the Aboriginal patriarch, Jim's boyhood friend, and his family.

Introduced by our friend Australian geomancer Julie Rocka and vouched for by Craig and Jim, we enjoyed treasured time with the elder and his extended family, who shared their home and sacred spaces with us.

The elder told us that he'd always lived on his ancestral land. Until recently, however, it had been a cattle ranch in the pastured tenancy of a white Australian farmer. Working for some years as a stockman on the ranch, the elder had endured awful treatment and often physical abuse. Seven times he had been run off the land and had even been thrown into jail for his insistence that this place belonged to him and his people and not the white usurpers.

When Europeans began to colonize Australia in the late 18th century, the land was legally assumed to be empty. For this principle to apply, however, the existence of the many tribal cultures comprising millions of Aboriginal peoples had to be denied. To further erase the Aboriginal heritage, for much of the 20th century white authorities were also legally able to forcibly separate Aboriginal children from their families. The tragedy of this 'lost generation' still ripples through the Australian psyche. Only in the last few years has this history of genocide been in some measure acknowledged and reparation effected. For the elder this has meant, in his old age, the return of the land of his ancestors.

The foundation of Aboriginal belief and culture, sometimes called the Dreamtime, is known to them as Tjukurpa. It is the spiritual heritage that pervades the entirety of Aboriginal life and weaves a seamless tapestry between the people, their environment and the wider Cosmos. It is a continuing co-creation, connecting the past, including the time when ancestral beings created the world, to the present and the future.

To 'prove' his heritage, with white anthropologists being the judges, the elder had to reveal his intimate knowledge of the Tjukurpa legends and the sacred places of his people. This he did, and the land was then restored to him and his descendants to enable them once more to be in spiritual and physical co-creative balance.

For us, to be welcomed into this world was a rare and precious opportunity to heal our own archetypal Tjukurpa connection with the Earth.

While staying with our Aboriginal friends, we learned that one important tradition is that they are not referred to by name following their death. They are then able to be free of the ties to this world. In writing of our time with them, I am honouring that tradition and so haven't named any of our hosts. This is a courtesy for the future and does not mean that their names and the memory of our time together will not continue to live on in our hearts. They do and will, forever.

*****

One morning, before it became too hot, we were all taken out into the bush by the wives of the elder and taught the women's business of recognizing edible plants and insects.

To our untrained eyes the bush appeared to be a harsh environment almost devoid of life. Yet, as we were shown, nondescript plants could provide a storehouse of food, and digging down into the soil could uncover an abundance of nourishing roots and grubs.

Three of us, with a great deal of huffing and puffing from the heat and effort, helped to dig up a magnificent specimen of a witjuti grub. Our efforts to prise up this single morsel of food gave us an insight into the fortitude and skill of our Aboriginal hosts.

As we were then slowly debating who should pluck up the courage to eat the white wriggling grub, one of our guides decided not to waste any more time and popped it into her mouth. Problem sorted.

The elder's trust in us was profound and we were taken to some of the sacred sites named in their Tjukurpa and introduced to their mythic meaning and significance. We deeply appreciated this opportunity to experience, with their custodians, some of perhaps the oldest continually revered places in the world.

On a hot afternoon we were led to a particular place of 'increase' where the Earth energies were very strong. Such energies, for those initiated into their secrets, can be worked with in many ways, for example to bring rain or increase the abundance of game. This particular place was a towering rock shelter whose walls were covered in red-ochre handprints. The prints were of two types – a solid print and an outlined one. The solid print was a mark to show that someone had passed that way; the outlined hand stated that an initiation had been undertaken here.

Knowing that the entire region had been suffering from drought conditions for many months, if not years, with the permission of the elder we attuned to the energies of increase to humbly ask the ancestral beings to send rain. Within a few hours, dark clouds had accumulated, but no rain fell. While grateful that the ancient ones had apparently heeded us, we realized that we clearly needed more practice in our communication with them!

Later that day, while camping by the river which flowed through the heart of this sacred area, we cooled off by playing in the waterhole with the Aboriginal kids, who were full of the joys of exploring life, like kids everywhere. We were told that the river was the pathway of Liru, the sacred serpent, and shown where to swim and where it was forbidden, as to do so would disturb him. No one in the Aboriginal family – not even the smallest or most mischievous youngster – would contemplate breaking such a mandate, as that would be deemed to bring physical and spiritual retribution on them personally and perhaps the entire family.

At night we slept in comfortable swag bags, open to the sky. This was much preferable to sleeping in tents, as here, many miles away from any other settlement, the sky was dark and the heavens awash with stars. One night, waking in the early hours, I gazed up in awe at the brilliant clarity of Orion and the Pleiades suspended above me.

The following evening, as we sat around the campfire, we asked the elder about the Aboriginal legends of the stars. He told us about Orion and how his people perceived the constellation as a mighty hunter. We were amazed to hear that their legends told of Orion stalking the sisters of the Pleiades, especially the youngest and most vulnerable of them. For this was virtually the same perception and legend told by the ancient Greeks and many other traditions around the world. Later, this archetypal legend would emerge in an unforeseen way during our journey to New Zealand.

The next day, as we said goodbye to each of our Aboriginal friends, our hearts were full. Holding and being held by each one in turn, I finally came to a dignified old man. He had been a quiet, gentle presence during our time with his family, often sitting a little apart but smiling at us as we went by. In his silent and graceful acceptance of life he reminded me of the old lady living on the reed island on Lake Titicaca.

As we looked deep into each other's eyes and held each other close, tears welled up in both our eyes and we allowed them to flow. Looking around, I felt immeasurably moved by the unspoken love that I could see we all felt for each other in that moment.

*****

Journeying on, we came to Yulara, the specially built resort that was to be the base for our exploration of the magnificent monoliths of Uluru and Kata Tjuta.

Uluru is a world-famous Australian icon. But far fewer people know of Kata Tjuta, which is only 20 miles distant. Its name means 'many heads' and refers to the cluster of 36 massive domes of red rock that rise spectacularly from the surrounding desert, dwarfing Uluru.

After the return of this land to its traditional Aboriginal owners, the Anangu people, it had been leased back to the Australian government as a national park. Now also recognized as a world heritage site both for its natural beauty and cultural importance, it was heartening for us to discover that it was managed by a board comprising six Anangu and four non-Anangu, guided by the traditional law of Tjukurpa.

Over the coming days, as we explored the essence of this primeval land, we too began to see and feel the archetypal embodiment of Tjukurpa pervade its every rock and sense the ebb and flow of powerful Earth energies beneath our feet.

The looming presence of Uluru rises over 1,000 feet above the surrounding plain, with sacred sites studded around its four-and-a-half-mile circumference. Many of its Tjukurpa stories, however, can't be shared. For a crucial aspect of this ancient knowledge is that it is only passed on as people are ready to take on the responsibility that accompanies such initiation. Many of the sites are thus only accessible to initiates, or are specifically restricted to women or to men, with unauthorized entry being perceived as desecrating their sanctity.

Looking up at the huge bulk of Uluru, I remembered that many of its Tjukurpa stories related to the enmity between the peaceful carpet snake people and the poisonous snake people, with many of the features around the monolith relating to their battles. As we too became enfolded by the land, we could now see how fissures in the rock bore testimony to the wounds of the warriors of both tribes and how certain stones formed the bodies of those killed. A rock, split and standing apart from Uluru, represented the nose of one warrior, hacked off in grief-stricken fury by the mother of one of his victims, and the cliff opposite embodied his ruined face, marked with the dark stains of water – his spilt blood.

*****

Although Uluru is the most famous sacred site in Australia, the guidance of the Elohim two years before was clear that the Soular Disc was energetically centred at Kata Tjuta. At that time I hadn't been aware of the significance of this amazing rock formation, whose size humbles its better-known neighbour. And only now did we become aware that the Aboriginal people consider Kata Tjuta to be even more sacred than Uluru.

Intending to spend the whole day exploring this place of power, we felt guided to hike the main trail into the heart of this sanctum, through the Valley of the Winds.

Meeting very few other people on the way, we quietly walked on, with the towering rocks around and above us making us feel tiny and yet safe and at home. We'd already felt male geomantic energy pervade Uluru and here we sensed a powerful female presence. Yet the Anangu initiatory places around Uluru are for women, while those at Kata Tjuta are for men. It seemed to us that the complementary energies of each would offer to their initiates an understanding of the opposite sex. At Kata Tjuta, men might gain deeper insights into female energy, whereas at Uluru the essence of male energy would be revealed to women. Given that we all embody both energies within us, what a wonderful way to achieve inner balance.

In the searing heat of the day, we could only walk slowly. For hour after hour, our entire sojourn within the embrace of Kata Tjuta was literally a moving meditation, both physically and spiritually.

Walking in silence, vivid images flitted across my inner and outer vision as I became aware of how much the landscape here was saturated with meaning. Without consciously knowing its Tjukurpa legends, I felt a familiarity with the stories held by these huge rocks. It was this sense of empathy, a feeling of archetypal belonging as old as the rocks themselves, which became the essence of our connection with the 6th Soular Disc.

The energies of the Disc flowed over and through me like a cooling and healing balm, not only at the times of our conscious attunements but with each breath and step. And as time ceased to have meaning, the process of its activation unfolded within our own hearts as we were enfolded within the heart of Kata Tjuta.

Bending down, I gently placed the small pebble from the portal of Amaru Muru in Peru onto the bed of the stream that meanders seasonally through this arid land. From here, the water would energize this tiny rainbow bridge, continuing the connection between each Disc as we journeyed on to activate the entire unity grid of Gaia.

As we climbed high above the Valley of the Winds to leave the inner environs of Kata Tjuta, I picked up another small pebble. Holding the resonance of the 6th Disc, it would journey with us to New Zealand.

But as we finally emerged, I sensed that the energies of the Disc were not yet fully activated and that we had more work to accomplish before leaving this Red Heart of Australia.

*****

The next day was free of any plans, but we all felt the call to connect more closely with Uluru.

Visitors are asked by the Anangu not to climb the sacred rock, as in accordance with traditional law only the initiated men of the tribe may do so. The Anangu call those who disregard this request and insist on making the long and dangerous climb *minga* – ants.

Agreeing not to be *minga,* we connected with Uluru by walking around it and attuning at the sacred places allowed us as non-Anangu. In caves, at waterholes and gazing at the ever-changing yet timeless stories held within the rock, we intuitively listened to its teachings.

As we connected more deeply with the landscape energies, our initial sense of the primacy of the male energy here strengthened and complemented the archetypal female presence of Kata Tjuta.

And yet something felt incomplete.

It was our last day in the Red Heart and we were browsing in the bookshop near our hotel. As we were to catch an early-morning flight the next day back to Sydney, this was our final opportunity to buy presents for friends back home.

Tony was looking intently at a postcard when he called me over. The card showed an aerial view of Kata Tjuta in the foreground and Uluru in the distance. Hardly visible on the far horizon was a tiny blip. To our amazement, we discovered that it was a third huge natural monolith, a flat-topped mesa rising out of the desert plain virtually in a straight alignment with the other two. It was called Aturla by the Aborigines and was also known as Mount Conner.

Excitedly we asked some local people about it, but no one seemed to be aware of its significance. While the iconic nature of Uluru has engendered the sharing of some of its stories with non-Aboriginal people, we had already discovered that very little of the Tjukurpa relating to Kata Tjuta was openly shared. And now we realized there was still less relating to Aturla.

The only legend we could discover relating to this third monolith was that it was the home of the Ice Men who roamed the landscape on cold nights, leaving frost as a mark of their passing. Intriguingly, the geology of this monolith, unlike that of Uluru and Kata Tjuta, is glacial debris dating back to an Ice Age millions of years ago.

If Uluru is perceived as geomantically embodying male energies and Kata Tjuta, female, Aturla should embody those of the cosmic child. As we attuned to its energies, we sensed that this was so. Again, synchronicity had been our way-shower to work with the reconciling energies of this cosmic trinity.

*****

It felt important for us to energetically connect with Aturla, but how?

Intuitively I associate the cosmic female principle with our heart, the cosmic male with our mind and the cosmic child with our will or purpose. The synchronicities that abounded through-out our journeys and our deepening energetic connection with the

8th chakra of the universal heart also continued to strengthen our sense that this portal to our higher awareness brought together the essence of our personal heart, mind and purpose to transcend the limitations of our ego-based awareness. So it was perfect that we were just able, in the time available to us before catching our flight, to return to Uluru at dawn the next morning.

We were guided to a particular sacred site there from where both Kata Tjuta and Aturla were visible. Standing together at the centre of the alignment, we looked towards Kata Tjuta and then in the opposite direction to Aturla. Joining hands in a circle, with coherent intention we envisaged the energies of this immense geomantic trinity being brought together and reconciled within the universal heart. Connecting again with the energies of the Soular Disc at Kata Tjuta, we then focused the combined energy down through our earthstar chakras beneath our feet and deep within the heart of Gaia to complete the activation of the Disc.

Later, back home, I read that the geomancer Robert Coon perceived Uluru and Kata Tjuta as the major aspects of the Earth's solar plexus chakra. According to Aboriginal lore, the entire continent of Australia is a macrocosm of the human body, with the Rainbow Serpent coiled within. Uluru, lying near its centre, is seen as the geomythic navel of the body, thus correlating with Coon's perception. And our energetic experience as we journeyed continued to be that the solar plexus chakra embodied the energies of our will, purpose and intention – the creative essence of the cosmic child.

I felt that we had been guided to a perspective in which Uluru and Kata Tjuta energetically supported Aturla, the geomantic solar plexus, for how otherwise could the cosmic child be empowered?

Again and again we were being reminded of the trinity that lies at the heart of so many spiritual and metaphysical traditions. When we talk about balance we most often perceive it as being that of the male and female cosmic principles which pervade the

Cosmos – the yin and yang of ancient Chinese teachings. Yet, as we were directly experiencing, the energy of the cosmic child needs to be an equal partner in our inner and outer healing.

I knew that our connection with the child energies at Aturla was continuing to encourage us to hear the voices of our children and their innocent wisdom and showing us how to liberate the creativity and purpose of the inner child within each of us.

*****

Flying back to Sydney for our ongoing journey, I reflected on what the Aboriginal elder had said about Orion and sensed the profound resonance of archetypal energies within the human psyche.

Archetypes hold the energetic essence of our collective experience and memory. They represent an original model or pattern of consciousness and in Carl Jung's pioneering work in psychoanalysis he postulated that archetypes were inherited mental images comprising our collective unconscious.

As we journeyed on, I was about to learn by vivid experience that while archetypes may emanate within the collective matrix of consciousness, they may also be embodied within an individual and within the land.

*****

A few days later, as we were driving into the beautiful Blue Mountains near Sydney, I felt terrible.

Having felt well and energized throughout the journey so far, I was shocked as throughout the day I became more and more exhausted, to the extent that by the time we arrived at our hotel I could barely shuffle my feet.

That evening, unable to eat, I lay quietly in our room. But as the hours slowly passed, my exhaustion refused to ease. As night fell and I lay there in the growing darkness, a flash of under-standing suddenly shot through me and I immediately regained all the energy that had drained from me.

I remembered that our driver had casually mentioned that the road we had taken that day had been built in the early years of colonial settlement by convict labour shipped out from England. Many of the convicts would have been in leg irons and literally only able to move by shuffling their feet. I now realized that I'd been physically embodying their collective energies, archetyp-ally held as an imprinted memory in the road built with their pain.

Recalling that European settlement of Australia in the 18th century began as a penal colony, I now began to sense its sad history. In harsh and unfamiliar conditions, the convicted workers suffered terrible deprivation, with many dying prematurely. Back in those days, deportation for life could be the sentence for merely stealing a loaf of bread. In the midst of convicts transported for serious and violent crimes were many whose sole 'crime' had been to try to feed themselves or their family.

As I remembered the convicts of Australia, the archetypal outcasts, I pondered on how we judge others and indeed ourselves.

Poignantly, the next day was Remembrance Sunday and we were able to attune to and hold a vigil to witness and support the healing of these traumatic birth pangs of Australia, whose effects still ripple in its psyche. As we did, we also shared a powerful sense of how our judgement of others and ourselves for what we consider to be convict behaviour so often prevents us from feeling empathy or compassion.

Later that day we drove back to Sydney and were able to go to the site of the first colony, where a three-sided statue commem-orates those who came here from across the world – settlers, soldiers and convicts. On one side of the statue is depicted a convict and as we looked down, we saw that his ankles were shackled with a pair of leg irons.

As our hearts overflowed with compassion, each of us said a silent prayer of healing to complete our work there.

*****

Our journey in Australia had begun to bring forward another level of healing – that of the archetypal aspects of our collective experience. Appreciating the incredible richness of our human consciousness, we wondered how this latest development would unfold as we continued on to New Zealand to activate the 7th Soular Disc.

Tony and I said goodbye in Sydney. Whatever the coming journey might bring forward for the group, we knew that it would be intensely personal for us and so we had both wished for him to continue on to New Zealand. But the journeys were proving to be a severe financial strain on our resources, and so, with reluctant acceptance, Tony left for home, where he would await my return.

As we acknowledged that nothing is without purpose and that I was meant to journey on alone, we could only trust that it would enable healing and the resolution of a pain that we had both learned was ancient and profound.

卐 卐 卐

CHAPTER 7

New Zealand

CHAPTER 7

NEW ZEALAND

November 2002

Though the Elohim had told me that the energies of the 7th Disc were centred on the South Island of New Zealand, its exact location was veiled from me until just before embarking on the journey there.

It seemed that either New Zealand, the land known to the Maori people as Aotearoa, 'the land of the long white cloud', was keeping something from me or I was keeping something from myself.

*****

Flying high above the waters of the Tasman Sea on our way to Auckland, I had time to mull over the journeys so far. We had now activated six of the 12 Discs. I was both relieved at how far we'd come and daunted by how far we'd yet to go!

When I had begun the journeys, I had been aware of their healing potential. At first I'd thought that this related to my fellow travellers and, through the activation of the Discs, that we could be in service to healing on a collective level. This had been validated by our experiences in Egypt and Africa.

But what was now emerging ever more emphatically was the role the Discs were playing in expanding our awareness and aiding us on profound and archetypal levels to re-member who we *really* are. It was a continuing energetic out-breath that was not only revealing our human and terrestrial heritage, but also our extraterrestrial origins and, step by step, our cosmic destiny.

The first glimpse of this had emerged when I'd asked the Elohim who they were and they had explained their ongoing mentoring of our Solar System and their direct involvement with the Soular Discs. In one incredible revelation, I'd found the wonder of the Universe arrayed across my inner vision in all its miraculous beauty. I'd felt that I was viewing the IMAX screen of creation, with a soundtrack provided by the Elohim.

As I had sat mesmerized by this vision, the Elohim had told me that the physical world was teeming with a vast array of Solar Systems, many similar to our own – an understanding that is gradually being appreciated by astronomers. Birthed from swirling clouds of gas and dust from the exploded remnants of previous star systems, each system is comprised of a central Sun and a family of encircling planets.

Each Solar System forms a matrix of consciousness, in essence a group soul, a Soul-ar System, supporting the evolution of life on many energetic levels. And for the entirety of its existence, each Soular System is assigned guardians, aetheric beings known to the ancients as the Watchers or Elohim. From our journeys so far, I'd now begun to realize that archetypal levels of our own consciousness are an intrinsic part of this group soul.

Our own Soular System was birthed four-and-a-half billion years ago. Physical life established itself here on Earth about 700 million years later, almost immediately after the planet had cooled sufficiently to allow water, the fundamental requirement of biological life, to liquefy.

The long history of our Soular System has seen vast stretches of time in which biological life has slowly evolved, interspersed by cataclysmic interludes. The Earth herself shows the scars of at least four of these, when almost all life here was obliterated. Yet each catastrophe held the seeds of a new beginning and the opportunity for life to develop in even greater diversity. Thus it was that the global cataclysm of 65 million years ago, which brought about the demise of the dinosaurs, enabled the mammals and ultimately us to become dominant on the Earth. And such periodic waves of birth, growth, death and rebirth have generated an incredible richness in the evolutionary exploration of consciousness.

The Elohim had gone on to explain that our collective human evolution is intimately connected with that of the living Earth and our Soular System as a whole, and also with other star systems and the entirety of our Milky Way Galaxy.

As is the case for individuals, a group soul too has a destiny, a purpose to its experience. The Elohim say that we are now at the time of an evolutionary leap in consciousness for our entire Soular System and the many prophecies of spiritual elders now converging are an intuitive and guided understanding of this.

When, 39,000 years ago, the Elohim gifted the Soular Discs to the initiates of ancient Lemuria, it was not for then, but for now. In these momentous times, the Discs are to be activated to help us to re-member who we *really* are and to inherit the cosmic destiny that we share with Gaia and the group soul that is our Soular System.

*****

From when I first learned of the gifting of the Discs to the Lemurian elders, I'd been curious to know whether I had been personally involved with them then. During my first year of asking, the Elohim gave no answer to this inner query. But then, in a series of spontaneous and shocking flashbacks and gentler assimilations, the story of that time was eventually given to me. Its trauma had been buried deep within my psyche and the greatest pain related to the shattering event that had culminated at the place I was now revisiting, the place of the 7ᵗʰ Disc.

This is my story:

Growing up, I had been aware of my psychic gifts from an early age, as had all the priestly initiates of my community. In those far-off Lemurian days, multi-dimensional realities were more easily accessed and extraterrestrial and intra-terrestrial contact common and openly acknowledged.

My own gifts were seen, however, as being exceptional, and by the age of 12, when I reached puberty, I was already being initiated into the more profound wisdom teachings. As was the custom, I was also betrothed to a boy of my own age who was also training in the priesthood. We were friends and fond of each other, both accepting the mandate of the elders.

Some time later, when we were married and had a child of about seven years old, the Soular Discs entered my life. Summoned by the high priest, I learned that I had been chosen as the oracle for the geomantic positioning of the 12 Discs around the Earth. I was to channel guidance from the Elohim, but someone else would be the geomancer who would understand their precise placements.

To energetically anchor each of the 12 geometric faces of the aetheric grid of the Earth so that they could be activated so far into the future, the location of the Discs required the alignment of telluric, elemental and cosmic energies. To facilitate the embodiment of unity consciousness within our human experience, they would resonate elementally with the creative Fire of spirit and the emotional Water of feeling. Connecting this shift of collective awareness with that of Gaia and of our entire Soular System also required their precise positioning to enable cosmic forces to be brought into future balance.

I was now introduced to the man who would work alongside me. I knew him, for he was the partner of a dear childhood friend. They too had been mandated to be together, like my husband and myself.

We would be away from our homes for three years. Before we left, my childhood friend, whom I loved as a sister, came to me. She felt that her relationship was fragile and asked me not to become emotionally involved with her partner. Without hesitation, I promised her that I would not.

Nevertheless, over the coming months, deeply committed to our joint task, the geomancer and I drew closer and closer, meeting each other on every level and recognizing each other as soul mates. Yet, in honouring the promise I had made to my friend, I refused to acknowledge the love I felt.

At the same time a shadow was stalking me as I went about making my preparations for each journey. While I barely knew the head of our priestly order, I could feel his growing interest in me. At first I thought he was keeping a fatherly eye on my work and inner development. Then one day, without warning or pity, he raped me.

Shocked beyond words at this betrayal of trust, I was also terrified of his authority. He knew without words the love I secretly held for my soul mate and had the power to expel us both from the order and the work we knew we were born to do.

When I realized I was pregnant, I felt as if my world was falling apart. I told no one and was now keeping two devastating secrets from my soul mate.

Unwilling to have the child and yet not able to confront any alternative, I punished myself. Our work required long and arduous journeying and I deliberately pushed myself to the limits of my endurance.

We eventually came to the land that would, many millennia into the future, be known as Aotearoa. The sequence in which we placed the Discs in that time was different from the order in which they would be activated 39,000 years later, and the Soular Disc of Aotearoa was the 12th and final one we placed all that time ago.

It was here that the tiny being that I held within me could no longer physically survive the self-inflicted rigour of my pain. My soul mate was my only companion and held me as I sobbed. Still unwilling to break my word to his partner, I could not tell him of the promise that imprisoned us all.

As if to ensure that everything was over, I suffered a final blow when word reached me that my own partner had died in an accident. Nothing could staunch the agony as I left my soul mate behind and made the long sad journey home.

Grief and regret were my constant companions throughout the rest of that life. My only solace was my prayer that thereafter I would find my soul mate again.

I never have until now.

Tony is my soulmate and had understood that I needed to travel to New Zealand without him to heal for both of us and for all those caught up in our ancient pain.

Without being consciously aware of it, every time I had sought to understand where the New Zealand Disc was, my inner sight had been clouded by the traumatic events of that distant time. It was only a few weeks before we were to travel to Australia and New Zealand that I was able to understand where the energies of the Disc were centred. It was in the heart of the sacred place known to the Maori people as Te Kohangi, their sacred birthplace of the gods.

The insight arrived courtesy of my friend Rona, who had come with us to Egypt for the first Soular Disc journey. At the time, she had wondered about her higher purpose for being there. It was only when we spoke of the 7th Disc being located in New Zealand, her home, that she understood that she was to be our way-shower.

Thanks to her, the location of the Disc was finally revealed and we were able to connect with the guides we needed during our journey. And while it seemed that Rona herself would be unable to join us, I had a glimmer of hope that she would.

*****

It was the Maori people who named New Zealand Aotearoa, 'the land of the long white cloud'. These Polynesian master navigators had settled here over 1,000 years before European sailors arrived in the 18th century.

The three-hour flight over the Tasman Sea from Australia reminded us of the remoteness of this beautiful land. With Tony and another of our Australian group having left for home and two other people about to join us in New Zealand, we would again be six in number and would be the first women-only group of the Soular Disc journeys. It seemed that both our number and gender were significant.

Arriving in Auckland, I quickly called two of Rona's contacts, geomancers Gary Cook and Michael Fleck. We'd heard from them about an ancient and enigmatic site near Rotorua in New Zealand's North Island named Te Miringa Te Karara, 'the Temple of the Four Winds'.

Both Gary and Michael travel extensively and are rarely at home, but when I called them on our arrival, they were able to see me later that afternoon. After I explained the purpose of our visit, we arranged to meet in a couple of days at the temple, which I was surprised and pleased to hear would be their first visit there too.

Te Miringa had been a Maori meeting-place, but it had been made of wood and had burned down in mysterious circumstances in the 1980s. According to those who had known it before its destruction, it had embodied multiple relationships of sacred geometry, ancient sacred measurement and cosmic alignment. To support its roof, 12 posts had been positioned in each of the four cardinal quarters, each representing a Maori elder, guardians of the wisdom of many realms. And at the centre had been a single post, the Arika, the conduit and integrator of the cosmic life-force.

Seeing once again this embodiment of 12 around 1 reminded me yet again of its fundamental nature as the harmonic of unity awareness, which, as I was beginning to glimpse, was the ultimate purpose of our journeys.

*****

Arriving at the Temple of the Four Winds, we paid our respects to its discarnate guardians and asked for their blessing.

Energetically, we all sensed that the land held a much older imprint than that of the Maori presence, that something was hidden beneath the ground and that Te Miringa had been built here in the knowledge of that ancient presence. But some of us also felt an immediate discomfort – something was way out of balance here.

Gary and Michael explained the layout of the temple, which was now merely outlined at ground level, and showed us where a pillar had been aligned to the star Alcyone, the youngest of the mythic seven sisters of the Pleiades star cluster.

As my mind returned to the Aboriginal legend of Orion stalking the Pleiades, especially the youngest and most vulnerable, I almost missed the next insight as Glyn, a local guide who had joined us, shared a story he had been told by two Maoris who had camped here one night.

In the middle of the night, one of the Maoris had woken up and seen a light shining in the area of the temple. When he went to investigate, what he saw was incredible. Two tall beings appeared to be taking crystals away from the temple. When he approached them, they telepathically communicated to him that they were from Orion and that the crystals would not be returned until the distorted energies present at the temple were healed.

Later, at our hotel, we shared our impressions of the day. Like Glyn, the two people who'd joined us in New Zealand knew nothing about our earlier discussion of Orion and the Pleiades. But for both of them, their attunement at Te Miringa had shockingly brought forward visions of the sacrifice of a young girl, perhaps 13 or 14 years of age, by an older man. It seemed that it had been a misguided attempt to reinvigorate the energies of the place, which had declined without the man or the other elders understanding the cause.

Both women had felt the energy of the sacrifice most strongly at the place where the pillar had been aligned to the Pleiades. Seeming to come from a very ancient time, long before the Maoris had arrived, it further strengthened our sense that Te Miringa was located at a site of much earlier significance.

As we brought all these threads of understanding together, we realized that the energetic archetype of the abusive male was, sadly, still prevalent in New Zealand. Christine, who had worked as a doctor in New Zealand some years before, told us that she'd often treated victims of domestic violence and knew that it was a substantial social issue here, despite an unwillingness to publicly acknowledge it as such. It now came as no surprise that it was she and the youngest woman of our group who had earlier experienced the sacrificial visions at Te Miringa. As we all now realized, this was the healing we were here to support.

We compassionately shared the ways in which relationships and trust between men and women have so often been unbalanced by predatory behaviour by both genders and the traumatic consequences compounded by a lack of acknowledgement and openness.

As we attuned together, we also intended and trusted that our healing work in New Zealand would support the rebalancing of the energies of Te Miringa Te Karara and the return of the crystals of Orion.

*****

For the following two days we based ourselves at Rotorua, the centre of the North Island and the heartland of the resurgent Maori culture. While honouring the Maori sacred knowledge, unlike our other journeys, where we had sought to work with local elders, we felt that to fulfil our purpose here we needed to connect with a much more ancient presence.

Rotorua is one of the most concentrated geothermal areas in the world and is now a spa town. The air is suffused with the acrid smell of sulphur arising from the many geysers and hot springs. Again, Fire and Water elementally energized us as we rested for a couple of days and walked amongst natural cauldrons of boiling mud, witnessing the precise timing in the release of boiling torrential geysers and luxuriating in hot pools warmed from deep within the Earth.

Next we journeyed on to the South Island. Based at Queenstown, on the shores of Lake Wakatipu, we'd arranged to spend a few days in the midst of some of the world's most gorgeous scenery – snow-capped mountains, verdant meadows and crystal-clear rivers and lakes.

Much of *The Lord of the Rings* trilogy was filmed here, and we revelled in the beautiful weather and spectacular landscape as we took time to explore the southern mountains and fjord-land of Milford Sound. In a strange way I felt our global journeys resonated with the films. Both offered the choice between fear and love. Both offered the possibility of a homecoming based on freedom and the claiming of one's birthright. It seemed synchronous that the final film of the trinity, *The Return of the King,* was to be released the following year at the exact time that we were to 'turn the master key at Avebury'.

*****

Our journey in Aotearoa was fast approaching its culmination as we drove over the Lindis Pass to the glacier-fed Lake Tekapo. Against a glorious backdrop of snow-tipped mountains, the bright turquoise of the lake arises from sunlight reflected off the myriad minute rock crystals suspended in its waters.

At the lake's edge, the tiny chapel of the Church of the Good Shepherd, built as a memorial to the European pioneers of the area, beckoned to us. As we sat quietly and gazed out at the peaceful vista of the lake, however, no inspiration for our purpose here came forward. Trusting that whatever understanding we needed to have would come in time, we left the church.

Suddenly, as we made our way over the grey-blue pebbles of the lakeshore, we all became aware of an enormous vortex of energy spiralling down into the water. In that moment we could sense the energies of the elemental alchemy of our journey being brought together in preparation for our connection to the Soular Disc the following day. Once again we realized that we needed to alchemically combine the elemental energies of Fire and Water – the Fire essence of the spiral energy with the elemental Water of the lake. They would then be poured into the grail of Fire that was the place where we would activate the energies of this Disc.

*****

After an overnight stay in Christchurch we drove to the area prosaically called Castle Hill, which lies about 60 miles west of the city as the land rises towards the great sweep of the Southern Alps. At the exact geographic centre of the South Island, this place is known to the Maori as Te Kohangi, 'the sacred nest', birthplace of the gods.

The land here is a basin formed of an ancient upthrust of limestone encircled by mountains hewn from schist and grewacke. Birthed in Fire, these igneous rocks create a grail for the Soular Disc's energies, which radiate powerfully throughout the Water-impregnated limestone.

Just before leaving home, I'd learned from Rona that to the Maori the stones of Te Kohangi reconcile children to their ancestral star systems, enabling them to be star walkers, free to roam the multi-dimensional realms of the Cosmos. And at this culmination of our journey, at the last minute, we were overjoyed that Rona was unexpectedly able to join us to activate the Soular Disc. As I'd hoped, our 7th sister had come forward for us to complete our healing of the archetypal trauma of Orion and the seven stellar sisters of the Pleiades by activating this 7th Disc.

When we shared the understanding of our purpose with Rona, she laughed – her sister's house is called 'The Seven Sisters'.

As we walked towards the great mass of rocks that formed Te Kohangi, we passed between two portal stones at its energetic threshold. Standing between them, I was about to say my name and ask a blessing for our work here when the aetheric guardians welcomed me by my Lemurian name, Mara'ana.

An ancient memory stirred within me and my gaze was drawn to an outcrop of rock some distance away. My heart stood still as I suddenly knew it to be the place where my soul mate Tony and I had experienced our deepest pain so many lifetimes ago. Seeing the place where our love had been torn apart, I could hardly breathe.

For both of us, other lives without each other had been shadowed in loneliness and grief and I realized that coming here again offered us the greatest healing the journeys had yet gifted us.

*****

Our seven sisters now clambered up to a small plateau within the embrace of Te Kohangi. Above us we saw and felt the presence of the guardian here, embodied in a great rock whose face was clearly visible. Powerful and benign, he held open the portal to the inner realms for us to do our work.

At Tekapo, we had vividly perceived an energetic vortex spiralling the Fire of our spiritual journey into the Water, the emotional body of the lake. Here, in the grail of Te Kohangi, two powerful vortices, one spiralling energy inwards and the other spiralling out, presaged both the completion of this stage of our inner and outer journeying and the birthing of the next.

As we came together to activate the 7th Disc, our highest intention was to honour and not abuse the vulnerability within ourselves and all other beings. We compassionately prayed and affirmed the release of all the pain of abuse, and I, weeping, gratefully felt the release of my own ancient grief.

As my own soul flew, liberated from the inner burden of remorse I had carried for so long, I sensed the activation of the Soular Disc and knew that its healing touched all who had played their part in that ancient Lemurian journey. I felt their ancient presence resonate with Te Kohangi and sensed that we were now ready to begin our journey back to the stars.

I realized too that to be whole we must be willing to be both strong *and* vulnerable – and that it is sometimes in our deepest vulnerability that our greatest empowerment is born.

Reverently, I left the tiny pebble brought from Kata Tjuta and chose another to carry on to Chile to connect with the 8th Disc, located in Antarctica.

And as I looked up into the clear blue sky, I knew that here, in this birthplace of the star children, we too had been reborn and that the future held a deeper understanding of our own cosmic destiny.

*****

Over the following months I offered myself space and time to integrate our amazing experiences.

Since the events of 9/11 the year before, I'd been feeling more and more strongly that both personally and collectively we were no longer able to sit on the fence and deny that we were part of an interconnected whole. I was now realizing that in continuing to undertake the Soular Disc journeys I was re-membering who I *really* am. Through the energetic portal of the 8th chakra of the universal heart, I was attuning to ever-higher levels of awareness that transcended my personality. And I began to see the patterns and preoccupations of my own and others' ego-based selves not with judgement but with compassion.

I was becoming consciously aware of the choices we all have every moment – choices of thought, feeling, word or action. I was experiencing, too, the increasingly immediate implications of my choices, both small and large. And at a deep level I was beginning to see how the energies radiating from those choices, at the most fundamental level either of love or of fear, were manifesting my realities.

Seeing my own inner choices writ large in the world events around me, I was unavoidably confronted by the truth that when we make choices of fear, they are ultimately choices to be separate. And when we choose love, we make the choice to be whole – within ourselves, with others and with the Cosmos.

The journeys were showing me and my fellow travellers, however, that we couldn't escape our human passions if we were to heal into wholeness. We were learning that our choices to love are only authentic when they honour and don't deny or ignore our fears. That it is only by embracing our fears wholeheartedly that we begin to heal the pain that birthed them.

The Elohim continued to guide and sustain me. And as the journeys continued to unfold, the understanding that we have incredible spiritual resources to call upon to collectively manifest unconditional love on Earth became an everyday reality.

But, as the elders say, 'we are the ones we've been waiting for'. It is our own personal commitment to embodying the passion of our own inner healing that is then able to resonate deep within the psyche of us all.

The journeys to come would continue to show, again and again, the truth of this empowering awareness.

*****

When we had arrived at Te Kohangi there had been a brief flurry of snow – a vivid reminder of the location of the 8th Disc. Arriving at the airport for our flights home, I giggled when I realized that the last thing I would see before leaving was a huge poster in the terminal building proclaiming: 'Antarctica, next stop'!

🏵 🏵 🏵

CHAPTER 8

Chile

CHAPTER 8
CHILE
March 2003

In the darkest hours of the night, fear gripped me.

Motionless in the world between dreaming and waking, I stood on a moonlit shoreline looking out into the vastness of the surrounding ocean. Transfixed, I saw a huge tidal wave, hundreds of feet high, rushing towards me. As the wave bore down on me, I was anguishing over all that I would lose.

Then, at the very last moment, as the wave was about to engulf me, I suddenly realized that my fear arose from this feeling of impending separation.

Just as suddenly, I became aware of separation as an illusion and *knew* at the very core of my being that there is no separation – ever! As the wave swelled forward, I willingly surrendered to its embrace and felt myself become one with it.

*****

The weeks leading up to my journey to Chile and then Easter Island to activate the 8th and 9th Soular Discs were riven by the impending invasion of Iraq.

Amidst a communal foreboding about the war, feelings of intensity and challenge deepened for me too as I sensed that my night-time vision might in fact be a premonition of what was actually to come – a premonition I felt unable to share with anyone, even and especially Tony.

As fears of what might be unleashed in the Middle East grew, it also began to seem that this would be the first Soular Disc journey that I would undertake alone, as understandably no one else seemed willing or able to come with me. The guidance of the Elohim was, however, distressingly direct. Whatever the reasons, and regardless of my concerns, I knew I must go, alone if need be, to activate the healing energies of the Disc.

And so, as I settled in for the long flight to Chile, my thoughts leaped forward to Easter Island, a tiny island in the vast expanse of the Pacific Ocean, still not knowing whether my unshared vision would materialize.

*****

Hitherto, the Elohim had been clear that manifesting the energies of the Discs required a physical human presence at the places where they were located. What I didn't understand was how the physical connection was to be made with the Soular Disc in Antarctica. For the Elohim had told me, over a year before the actual journey, that we could activate it from Chile instead of travelling to Antarctica itself. Why was this journey different?

During the flight, I reflected on the events that had unfolded in the past few days. To connect with the Antarctica and Easter Island Discs, I'd arranged to fly from England to Santiago, Chile, where in a way yet to be revealed and in accordance with the guidance of the Elohim, I trusted that I would connect with the Antarctica Disc. I'd then planned to fly on to Easter Island the next day. Given that it seemed I would journey alone, I intended to focus wholly on the activation of the Discs and so arranged the tightest itinerary I could, a round journey of nearly 19,000 miles in less than seven days.

Anita, who had journeyed with us to Africa and Alaska to activate earlier Soular Discs, had then e-mailed me to say that she'd been guided to join me, without really understanding why.

At this last moment, grateful for a travelling companion, I breathed a sigh of relief.

In her first e-mail Anita had told me that she planned to meet me on Easter Island, intending only to land in Santiago to change flights. Well, that was the plan! The Cosmos had other ideas. A further flurry of e-mails charted her attempts to obtain flights without success. Eventually, the only flight she could arrange required her to arrive early in Santiago, stay overnight there with me and for us both to catch the next morning's flight to Easter Island. It meant that we would be together in Santiago to activate the Antarctica Disc before flying on to activate the Easter Island Disc.

Anita then gave me the news that explained everything – and confirmed, in a wonderful way, the guidance of the Elohim. She e-mailed that she'd visited Antarctica some years before. I suddenly realized why we'd be able to activate the Antarctica Disc from Chile and why we needed to be there together – Anita would act as the physical bridge to the Disc with her previous, albeit unconscious, connection with it.

When we met in Santiago, we were amazed to discover that she had travelled to the exact place which the Elohim had given me as the Disc's location – just under the Antarctic ice-sheet almost directly south of the tip of South America. Neither of us had known of this incredible synchronicity before our discussion in Santiago.

Of my many travelling companions, Anita was the only one who could energetically work with me to activate this 8th Disc from where the Elohim has said it could be done – and here we were, destined to be together.

*****

Arriving in Santiago on 8 March, I took a taxi to the hotel, passing on the way the long line of a peace march protesting about the imminent war in Iraq. Seeing the large number of protesters here, at the southern tip of South America, I appreciated how widespread the global fears were about this coming war and its unforeseen consequences.

Before leaving England, I'd sent the following letter to all those who were spiritually supporting the Soular Disc journeys:

> Each journey is offering opportunities to co-create healing on individual, collective and archetypal levels.
>
> The possibility of war in the Middle East and the continuing 'war against terrorism' offer us choices of love. It is the divine feminine essence within all of us whose voice can be raised now to find another way from that which humanity has pursued in the past. We can speak out now for a profound healing of the perceived differences which have been at the root of the impetus to war through the ages.
>
> On collective and geomantic levels, we may perceive Antarctica as holding the essence of ice-soulation. Such isolation within our human family has separated us from each other – nation, creed and colour – for millennia.
>
> As we open our hearts, we can melt the ice and allow the water of emotional freedom to flow.
>
> As we connect with the 8th Soular Disc on 8 March, we invite you to feel the energy of the 8th chakra of the universal heart.
>
> The healing of the ice-soulation between us, I believe, enables the divine female essence, powerfully present on Easter Island, to connect with, balance and free the fear patterning of the predominantly male energies in the nexus of the Middle East.

Anita and I invite you to join us in co-creating rainbow bridges of meditation and prayer at the times we will be connecting with the Soular Discs whose energies hold the vibration of unity consciousness and unconditional love.

We en-courage you to open your heart joyously, as a conduit for unconditionally loving harmony to manifest collectively on Earth.

As I wrote the letter and prepared for this journey, I thought about how often we choose emotional isolation as a perceived protection against pain. Sometimes our fear is that if we empathize with others we will drown in their pain. At other times we recognize that their pain will open the floodgates of our own – dammed and held suppressed maybe for years, or entire lifetimes.

But isolation only gives the illusion of protection – in reality it is imprisonment, the isolation of our soul – our ice-soulation. Until we make the choice to melt our isolation, we remain prisoners, unable to fully express what it means to be human, unable to feel kinship with others and ultimately unable to love.

Our ice-soulation has enabled us to diminish our common humanity and has supported and driven acts of warfare throughout history. In the past, we have allowed ignorance and fear of other cultures to fester prejudice and separation. If we continue to exclude rather than include all the members of our human family, we will continue to repeat these patterns of history.

I knew that somehow this journey would play a part in healing our collective pain.

*****

Sunset was approaching as we sat down on a park bench in the Parque de Forestal in the centre of the bustling city of Santiago.

Behind us an ancient tree hugged the ground and the sound of children's laughter rippled from a nearby playground.

As we attuned ourselves to the energies of the Disc, I envisioned the incredible ice-green depths of the Antarctic Ocean far to the south. With my inner vision, I saw the Soular Disc, a beautiful lens of white gold light suspended in the water below the icecap.

Unlike my experiences of activating the other Discs, which had been unaccompanied by aetheric guardians, here I perceived eight beings in a circle, facing and surrounding the Soular Disc. They seemed human-like in form but able to breathe and be fully at ease beneath the water. I also sensed their acknowledgement of Anita and me and knew that their presence was to join with and augment our energetic intention for the Disc's activation.

Focusing my awareness on my 8th chakra, I surrendered myself to the universal heart of the Cosmos, allowing all sense of ice-soulation to melt away. Gently and effortlessly, as I felt myself freed from the ancient imprisonment of my own making, I saw the Disc majestically rise through the water and break through the icecap. As it did so, a vertical column of brilliant light radiated from both its upper and lower faces, reaching high into the sky and down into the ocean depths. I knew the energies of the Disc were now activated.

Anita too had clearly seen the column of light emanating from the activated Disc.

Connecting with its loving energies, I now felt able and willing to empathize with and understand the pain of others, and indeed my own, at a more profound level, recognizing that it is our fear and pain that so often motivate us.

In whatever small way, as each of us melts the coldness of our own ice-soulation, we contribute not only to our own inner peace but also to the peace of the world.

🕉 🕉 🕉

CHAPTER 9

Easter Island

EASTER ISLAND

March 2003

The next day, I nestled into my seat as our plane took off for the five-and-a-half-hour flight over the ocean to the speck of land that is Easter Island.

Almost immediately, I felt a strong surge of anger rise up through me. As I asked myself what this powerful feeling was all about, I saw with my inner vision first one and then a second scenario in my past. In both cases, I'd taken decisions that had resulted in difficult and costly outcomes for both others and myself. I had thought I'd already forgiven myself and those concerned and released the pain of those scenarios, but clearly my emotions were giving me a different message.

Over the next hour I continued to sit with the anger, allowing it to swirl within and around me. Finally I felt my emotions pause, as if for breath. Very quietly, so that I could hardly hear it, a small inner voice said, 'You heard, but you didn't listen.'

Understanding dawned on me. I remembered how in each scenario my intuition had warned me not to go ahead with what I then had done – with all the trauma that ensued.

My initial anger had been directed at others for behaving badly and at myself for being 'stupid'. That was long since dissipated. But what I'd been unable to acknowledge and forgive was that I had heard my inner guidance and then not listened to it. Worse still, I had actively suppressed it.

With that awareness I suddenly felt an overwhelming compassion, and true forgiveness for myself and those concerned flowed through me, unforced and heart-felt. As tears rolled down my cheeks, I knew that this aspect of personal healing was somehow crucial to the work we would do on Easter Island – the need to both hear and listen and then to speak and act with the loving truth of our inner voice.

As I also recalled the letter I had written before this journey and how I felt that the inner voice of the divine feminine within all of us might now be raised in service to peace and reconciliation, I now realized that I had needed to find this inner peace and reconciliation within myself first.

*****

Due to the limited number of flights to and from Easter Island, on our arrival Anita and I had a day and a half before our dawn connection with the Soular Disc. We felt that the best way to orientate ourselves and gain a geomantic understanding of the island and the energies of the Disc was to sign up for an afternoon tour. With no time to lose, we arranged to join a group a few hours after our arrival.

The weather was balmy with a slight breeze as we arrived at our first stop, the dormant volcanic crater of Rano Kau. As we stepped toward its rim, Anita and I looked at each other. Without words, we both knew that this was where we would experience the Soular Disc's energies at their most powerful.

The crater, created by the fiery outpouring of lava from deep within the Earth, now formed a grail for rainwater, vital to the islanders in this place without rivers. And again I was reminded of the energetic mandala of every Disc – the elemental presence of Fire and Water.

Standing on the rim of the crater, I gazed across the vastness of the Southern Ocean towards Antarctica. And on the wind coming from its icy reaches came the words: 'Hear our voices, hear our voices.'

Walking on towards the ceremonial village at the crater's southernmost point, we discovered that the name of this sacred place – Orongo – meant 'the place to hear and listen'!

For the remainder of our short time on Easter Island, I opened myself to the whispers of its past and the voices of its ancestors in order to reveal the song of its present and be in service to the healing of its future.

*****

Easter Island lies at the eastern vertex of Polynesia, which, together with New Zealand to the south-west and Hawaii to the north, forms an enormous triangle laid over the Pacific Ocean. The many islands dotted throughout this vast region are perceived as the last vestiges of sunken Lemuria. Indeed, legend says that thanks to their great protective deity Make-Make, the Polynesian people, the first to settle on this remote island, were able to escape to it when their motherland sank beneath the waves of the ocean.

The Polynesian settlers discovered an abundant and stable ecology that supported a rich rainforest and copious bird life. Introducing plants and animals of their own, though, they immediately began to clear the forest to plant crops. Perhaps continuing their ancient ways, modest ceremonial platforms were also constructed and small statues erected on them. The population grew steadily and about 1,000 years ago more and bigger platforms began to be built and more and larger statues, or *moai*, to be erected on them.

The forest was cleared not only to provide land for crops but also to provide timber rollers and sleds to move the statues and the wood for cremation rites for the dead. As resources dwindled, it appears that yet more statues, even larger than before, were erected. Within 500 years, population growth and deforestation had led to a catastrophic ecological disaster and population collapse.

As we heard the settlers' tragic story, Anita and I reflected on how it could be seen as a microcosm of what was happening to the entire Earth.

*****

Ever since its discovery by Europeans in the 18th century, the island has been famous for its enormous and enigmatic statues, or *moai*. These *aringa ora*, or living countenances of the ancestors, are the greatest legacy of a complex and sophisticated culture.

Over 200 massive statues were moved considerable distances from where they were quarried and were erected on stone platforms forming an almost unbroken ring around the edge of the island. It is as though the island is crowned by a geomantic and giant stone circle of protection. Almost all the ancestor statues stand with their backs to the ocean, overlooking, guarding and guiding the villages clustered around them.

Standing in front of the imposing array of *aringa ora* at the platform of Tongariki, I began to hear their voices. The statues remaining in the quarry were, to me, silent. But those of the living ancestors around the island spoke clearly. It was only later that I understood that this might have been because their energetic activation was only brought about by the ceremonies that accompanied their raising and dedication to their communities.

Throughout that day, around the island, ancestor after ancestor told me their story:

> Easter Island had initially been discovered by explorers and then four great catamarans, well supplied to colonize this remote place, had braved the long journey to its rocky coasts.

For many generations thereafter, the bounty of the sea, land and air had gifted the islanders with abundant lives. One year, however, the climate changed. The fishing grounds were depleted and the crops failed.

The next year, there was no respite and many of the islanders slid into fear. There were some who heard their inner voices encouraging them to trust and to find different ways of surviving through this time. The voices of fear, however, were loud, and it was to those that the community listened.

Statues of the ancestors began to be raised to intercede with the gods, who were perceived as sending this catastrophe. When conditions failed to improve, the voices of fear insisted that the statues weren't impressive enough and that the ancestral powers embodied in the *aringa ora* were insufficient. Larger and then still larger statues were needed, at an ever-increasing cost to the fragile resources of the island.

When environmental conditions eventually eased, the voices of fear continued to speak, saying that only by raising more and still larger statues could a future catastrophe be averted. So resources became more and more depleted, until the last tree was felled and the islanders were unable even to build canoes to fish or to escape. Fear had brought them to the brink of the destruction they so feared.

The ancestors' grief at hearing but not listening to the guidance of their inner voices reflected my own. I now grieved with them, releasing the pain without judgement and embracing the deeper understanding it had brought. As I acknowledged their experiences, I asked what Anita and I could do to help them heal.

I reflected how the ecological disaster of Easter Island held many lessons for all of us to urgently understand today. We too have a rampantly expanding global population and are aggressively destroying our environment. In this tiny island in a vast ocean of water, can we see the reflection of our entire Earth, a tiny island in the vast sea of space?

It was only later that I understood what might have been the cause of the catastrophe that the ancestors spoke of. Some 600 to 700 years ago it appears that a climatic disaster did occur. For several generations, the weather was dramatically colder – what has been called a 'little Ice Age'. Crops would have withered and bird and sea life suffered – exactly what the voices of the ancestors had described.

The catastrophe impacting an already unstable and fragile situation brought about the collapse of nearly a millennium of peaceful co-existence. No more statues were carved and the lack of wood saw cremation of the dead giving way to burial. The archaeological record shows that enormous quantities of weapons made from obsidian – dark volcanic glass – were then made. Violence had shattered the peace.

Our guide, Teringa, then told us that finally, in despair, the statues were all toppled and this once abundant society almost destroyed itself.

Yet the abandonment of the extremes of the islanders' ancestral religion and the breakdown of their existing social system ultimately became their salvation. At Orongo, the ceremonial village high on the cliff between Rano Kau and the ocean, a new tradition was created by the choice of an annual chief, the *tangata manu* or birdman.

Teringa told us that each of the candidates for chief nominated a young champion. It was he who would brave the challenge to climb down the sheer 1,000-foot cliff to the shore and swim a mile through the strong currents and shark-infested waters to the islet of Moto Nui.

Here, for perhaps weeks, the champions would await the arrival of a migratory sea bird, the *manutara* or sooty tern, poignantly now no longer a visitor to the island. The winning champion was the one who retrieved the *manutara*'s first egg, swam back through the dangerous waters and climbed the high cliff to deliver it safely before the assembled congregation.

As we had discovered, Orongo means 'the place to hear and listen'. It seems that those who derived the birdman ritual as a means of defusing violence and enabling the island's society to become once more sustainable had indeed heard and listened.

To symbolize the balance between the change and continuity of the Easter Islanders' society, a great statue, Hoa Haka Nana Ia, was erected at the centre of Orongo. Uniquely carved from basalt rather than the softer rock of the other island statues, it appears from the front to be a classic *moai*, while on its back is carved the birdman. This great symbol of survival was pillaged from the island and now stands in the British Museum in London. It is believed that the last ever birdman ceremony was performed at Orongo only a short time before the statue was taken.

Perhaps one day, as a mark of our own commitment to reconciliation, the statue will be allowed to return home.

*****

My own visionary experience of the huge wave returned that day too, as Teringa told us of the tidal waves that had from time to time swept over the island.

In 1960 an earthquake had devastated the south of Chile. Two thousand miles away, the resulting tsunami had swept over the eastern shore of Easter Island, carrying away everything in its path and scattering the great statues at Tongariki as if they were children's playthings.

With a great sigh of relief I now realized that my terrifying night vision had not been a premonition but a resonant memory

I shared with the ancestors. This understanding now helped me to empathize with the overwhelming fear that had brought them to the brink of oblivion.

I could now sense that the ancestors would be joining Anita and me to support Easter Island's healing and to release our collective ice-soulation by our activation of the Soular Disc the following day.

*****

Early in the pre-dawn chill of the next morning Anita and I returned to the crater of Rano Kau, where we had felt the energies of the Soular Disc so powerfully. We settled down quietly on its inner slope and attuned ourselves to our purpose.

As I surrendered myself to being a channel for the loving energy of the Soular Disc to be activated, brief memories of the last few days played across my mind's eye. I was profoundly grateful that my ongoing healing and inner work before leaving home, in Santiago, on the flight to the island and the previous day had prepared me for this connection. I knew, at a deep level, that had I not been able to heal my own pain from the times when I had heard but not listened to my inner guidance and thus achieve my own inner peace and reconciliation, I would not have been able to make my connection to the divine feminine and the Disc in service to our collective healing.

Anita and I began our attunement by energetically connecting to the ancestors of Easter Island, the Discs already activated and all those around the world who were journeying with us in Spirit. In the universal heart of the 8th chakra, we opened ourselves to the divine feminine presence within every one of us. Our only intention was to be clear channels to hear and listen to her voice in our own lives.

Exactly 13 minutes later, as our attunement completed its purpose, I opened my eyes to see the Sun just emerging over the rim of the crater and flooding it with white-gold glory. The 9th Soular Disc had been activated.

Anita and I were too overcome to do much more than hug each other in joy and gratitude.

*****

On arriving back in England and learning of the experiences of the others who had taken part in the activation, I discovered that a number of us had multi-channelled a double aspect of the divine feminine. In envisaging the activation of the Disc, we had each perceived the receptive aspect of our inner voice, represented by the essence of Water coming into wholehearted balance with the creative energy of Fire to then manifest its truth.

I now realized that individually and collectively, our ability to hear our inner voice was becoming stronger. Our ongoing choice and challenge is to be willing to listen to it and to speak and lovingly enact the integrity of our inner truth.

We are offered the gift of this choice above all in our closest relationships. It can be so easy to avoid speaking our truth for fear of hurting those we love. Or, in desperation and frustration, we may blurt out truth without love. And yet, when we are willing and able to speak our truth lovingly, from the heart, its healing essence is transformational.

*****

Our next journey would be to Hawaii at the summer solstice. Here we would be embraced by its ancient culture of *aloha* and the living reality of loving truth in relationship.

Eighteen months before, a solar eclipse had traced an arc of totality over the Pacific Ocean from Easter Island to Hawaii, reaching across the enormous area that had once been Lemuria. Astrologers had perceived the Lemurian eclipse as offering the transformational release of very ancient emotional and power patterns which had pertained then and which had since been held energetically within the planetary grid. Considered a deeply transformative eclipse, it had challenged us to bring the empowerment of our intention into alignment with spiritual values and love in our relationships, especially those closest to us.

Significantly, the eclipse had occurred in the constellation Ophiuchus, the cosmic healer, whose location marks the centre of our Galaxy – a recurring theme in many astrological alignments since 1999 and a connection that was to emerge as being crucial to our understanding of our cosmic destiny.

All solar eclipses have a continuing wave of influence. And following my journey to Easter Island in March, Tony and I both felt that to complete the effects of the Lemurian eclipse by releasing those ancient patterns and aligning with the new energy, we needed to be together in Hawaii.

We also hoped that this would complete the healing of our emotional trauma from that ancient lifetime together and support our collective healing of those Lemurian patterns of relationship.

✻ ✻ ✻

CHAPTER 10

Hawaii

CHAPTER 10
HAWAII
June 2003

Before leaving for Hawaii, I'd experienced three extraordinary 'galactic' visions within the space of a few days.

In each of these, I was standing out in the almost unimaginably vast depths of intergalactic space with our own Galaxy, the Milky Way, stretched across my full field of view. Against the midnight blackness of space, its radiance was exquisite and I could see with crystal clarity the myriad colours of stars and exquisite veils of interstellar gas clouds spiralling within it.

The strangest aspect of the experience was that I still appeared to be physically in my human body. I could actually feel my feet standing on a transparent yet solid platform and distinctly hear and feel my breathing. In all my years of etheric travelling throughout multi-dimensional realms of consciousness, this was the first time I'd brought my physical body along with me!

Normally during these spiritual sojourns, my awareness expands and I've rarely felt daunted by my experiences or by the multi-dimensional beings I have encountered. But this was very different. I felt tiny amidst the vastness of the Universe that surrounded me and at first, overwhelmed by what was happening, I began to hyperventilate.

Then I became aware of four beings just outside my field of vision. As I heard one laughingly say to the other, 'It's all right, she'll stop soon,' I began to calm down.

Almost immediately, the vision ended. The two that followed were equally vivid and equally brief. But the fleeting experience of each enabled me to feel a little more at home in this extraordinary new way of perceiving my own place in the Cosmos.

While I had heard no direct message, I had a powerful sense that what I'd so profoundly experienced was connected to our forthcoming journey to Hawaii and to my unfolding understanding of the Elohim's message about turning the 13th master key at Avebury on 23 December 2003.

*****

The Hawaiians call their islands Pihanakalani, 'the place where Heaven meets Earth'. These islands are indeed set like radiant jewels in the embrace of what seems a never-ending ocean.

My guidance from the Elohim was that our journey should begin on the island of Kauai and then move on to Maui to activate the 10th Soular Disc at the ancient volcano of Haleakalā. They also guided that the specific timing of the activation should be sunset on the solstice of 21 June 2003.

As usual, I had little prior understanding of why this itinerary or time and date was important. But I trusted that time would tell.

As Tony and I flew from San Francisco to Kauai to meet the rest of our group, I sat and pondered. Both this flight and my previous journey to Easter Island involved flights of more than 2,000 miles over the Pacific Ocean to the most distant inhabited islands on Earth. Like Easter Island, the Hawaiian group is formed of the tips of enormous volcanic mountains reaching up nearly four miles from the floor of the Pacific Ocean. Hawaii is the northern point of the huge triangle of the Polynesian Islands, the vestiges of the empire of Lemuria. Our journey to Hawaii was thus completing a trinity of Soular Disc activations which had begun in New Zealand and continued on Easter Island. Allied to the energies of the 'Lemurian' eclipse, this third journey appeared to be the culmination of a healing of ancient Lemurian consciousness and the integration of the new energies birthed by the eclipse.

And yet again we were to discover that the Disc intimately embodied the elemental archetypes and balance of Fire and Water.

*****

The essence of Hawaii is *aloha*. This Polynesian word describes the ancient spirit of nurturing and hospitality that embraced us like a warm breeze when we arrived on the garden island of Kauai. As we were greeted by our dear friend Wendy, who'd arranged our pilgrimage, the island too felt like an old friend welcoming us home.

Bathed by a glorious sunset, we gathered on the beach at Anahola, on the eastern coast of the island. It is here that the Hawaiians say that all human souls physically incarnate before moving on to their chosen family.

And here we met Puna Kalama Dawson, a *kahuna,* a priestess of the Hawaiian tradition, able to move between the worlds of spirit and matter. Puna, of the Old Hawaiian royal lineage, and her group follow the ways of *huna*, the ancient tradition of Hawaiian spirituality expressed through the sensuous dance of the *hula*.

After years of suppression, the spirituality of Polynesia is now re-emerging. Its native wisdom, thanks to Puna and others like her, is becoming accessible to those non-Hawaiians who feel the spiritual call of these ancient lands.

Later, as the Sun was setting, we offered fragrant *lei* of tropical blossoms to Pele, the powerful goddess of volcanoes, asking her blessing on our purpose and journey.

*****

The next morning we were up early to greet the Sun in the traditional Hawaiian way. Arriving at Wailua beach, we quietly joined Puna and her group for a special dawn ceremony.

The Hawaiians train themselves to look directly at the Sun as it rises, believing that its therapeutic powers are greatest at this time. We sat in a long row facing the horizon, and as the Sun began to appear above the ocean, Puna began a sonorous Hawaiian chant, clapping to keep time:

E ala e, ka la i ka hikina,
I ka moana, ka moana hohonu,
Pi'i ka lewa, ka lewa nu'u.
I ka hikina, ae a ka la.
E ala e.

Awaken, arise the Sun in the east,
From the ocean, the ocean deep,
Climbing to the heaven, the heaven highest.
In the east, there is the Sun.
Awaken.

Everyone joined in as the Sun, a dazzling vibrant orange, slowly rose in the sky.

The chant to welcome the Sun must continue until its full orb is seen, and if the day is cloudy, that might take some time!

As we welcomed the Sun, the clouds hugged the horizon and the Sun rose majestically into the clear blue sky.

*****

Nurtured by Kauai's gentle energies, each day blossomed like the bougainvillea spilling abundantly all around us. Our journey flowed easily and our group rapidly became family.

One of the greatest joys that Kauai gifted to us was Krish, who cooked for us throughout our stay on the island. Arriving each morning laden with magnificent fruit and vegetables from the market, he nurtured our bodies with his wonderful food and our hearts with his presence. His loving energy continued to enrich us as we explored Kauai and experienced its magic. In the Chinese symbol for yin and yang, the seed of yin arises within the yang and vice versa. With Krish, we gratefully received daily reminders that the seed of the 'extraordinary' arises from the 'ordinary' times we share.

One morning, driving to the furthest extent of the northern coast road, we arrived at paradise. A tiny beach of pure white sand greeted us and the gentle lapping of the turquoise sea welcomed us into its warm embrace. We laughed and played against the tropical backdrop of a cliff overhanging with luxuriant life and known to the ancient Hawaiians as Makana – 'the gift'.

Nearby was a temple, or *heiau*, dedicated to Laka, the goddess of *hula*. In years gone by this was the location of Kauai's most sacred *hula* school, to which aspiring students would come from all over the Hawaiian Islands.

Sunset was approaching as we walked beneath the almond trees and along the cliff path to the temple. Climbing beyond its first enclosure, where night-time *hula* is still performed on special occasions, we continued to the highest enclosure, which is close to the cliff and overlooks the ocean.

We each settled down facing the setting Sun and gave thanks for this precious day. As we did so, a gentle benediction of warm rain began to fall. No one moved as it passed over us, its pure fresh water mingling with that of the ocean, still damp on our bodies.

*****

The following evening, as I looked out from our room to the lush gardens that surrounded us, I became aware of two groups of beings standing silently by the trees. In the twilight, I could see that each group was comprised of three beings. Those of the first group were small and slight. They were earthy skinned and their energy felt shyly elemental. The others, standing a little apart, were pale and much taller.

While I recognized the taller beings as Lemurian, I'd not encountered the smaller beings before. Feeling that all six welcomed us here, I also sensed that the smaller beings were specifically asking us to acknowledge them and to include them in our work.

Later, as we heard and read the ancient Hawaiian stories of the beings that had inhabited these islands before the Polynesian peoples came, I realized who our small visitors were. Many Hawaiian legends refer to them as the Menehune and describe them as being skilful engineers of stone monuments, some of which stand to this day.

Archaeologists, however, believe that people from the Marquesas Islands, far to the south, probably settled Kauai from about 1,500 years ago. When the Polynesian people arrived here about 1,000 years ago, it appears that they subjugated the Marquesas people, forcing them to build the temples and irrigation ditches now attributed to the Menehune. As the Polynesian word for 'outcast' is *manahune*, it is thought that this refers to the social diminishment of the Marquesas people becoming legend.

The energies of the Menehune that I'd seen in the garden, however, felt elemental rather than human and more ancient than the Marquesas people. Perhaps, in legend, the social diminishment of the Marquesas had somehow become overprinted on a much earlier memory of the original Menehune?

*****

The spirit of *aloha* welcomes all spiritual traditions to the islands. Hearing of the Kadavul Hindu temple on the banks of the Wailua river, we planned to visit it.

This sanctuary was envisioned by its venerated founder, Gurudeva, as a temple of *kaivalya*, offering freedom from the past and a vision for the ultimate attainment of the Self within man. It is also home to one of the largest quartz crystals in the world, weighing 700 pounds and estimated to have taken 50 million years to become its perfected form. In the Hindu tradition, it is venerated as offering spiritual wish-fulfilment. Crystal healers such as Katrina Raphael, the founder of the crystal academy on Kauai and author of *The Crystalline Transmission,* have identified it as one of 12 Earth-keeper crystals now being activated around the world.

Katrina perceives the role of the Earth-keeper crystals as two-fold: to transmit the accumulated knowledge of the physical plane of the Earth to support the development of consciousness in other stellar realms, and to be a conduit for higher spiritual inspiration to reach the Earth plane. The 12 Earth-keepers thus play their role at this time, as do the 12 Soular Discs, both correlating with the 12-fold aetheric grid of Gaia and the re-membering of our own 12-fold chakra system.

We were welcomed into the peaceful surroundings of the Kadaval temple and were gently ushered into the sanctum, where a Hindu monk was gracefully presenting offerings and prayers. He kindly invited us to join him.

After the ceremony, I felt a sense of anticipation. I remained cross-legged on the floor, waiting for something that now felt ready to unfold. Before I had left on this journey, for the first time the Elohim had guided me to bring my Lemurian record-keeper crystal. Such crystals are perceived as storing ancient knowledge and profound cosmic understanding and each calls to the person it is meant to work with.

Since calling me several years before, my crystal had been resolutely silent, as though waiting for the perfect place and moment to activate and reveal its wisdom. Now, sitting facing the great Earth-keeper crystal for what seemed an age and feeling increasingly cramped and uncomfortable, I found my inner guidance was nonetheless telling me to wait and see.

Cradling my Lemurian crystal in my cupped palms, I suddenly felt it resonate with the energies of the Earth-keeper. At the next moment – literally between breaths – my consciousness exploded.

Expanding to the scale of a Galaxy, I could feel myriad life-forms spiralling within me – stars, planets and beings of all shapes, sizes and awareness. This was completely different from my three previous galactic visions. Then I had been in human form looking out at the Milky Way; now I became the mind of an entire Galaxy. Then I had felt tiny; now I felt vast.

When I'd first begun to receive the guidance of the Elohim, I had been eager to understand as much as I could. They had gently told me that understanding would be given to me gradually, as otherwise the scale of it would be overwhelming. It was only over time, as the journeys progressed, that I came to fully appreciate their compassion and wisdom.

Now, as I began to perceive the huge impact of what was unfolding, I realized that I would have been unable to deal with its enormity without experiencing, step by step, all that had gone before. The human part of me could feel my body and emotions reacting – my mouth was dry and my stomach churning. But my greater awareness felt calm and accepting, and I sensed at the very heart of my being that I was experiencing a homecoming.

At that moment, I realized my destiny was to bring the wholeness of all that I really was through my human experience – and I knew that it is a cosmic destiny we all share.

*****

Driving up into the hills to enjoy the glory of the Full Moon rising above the ocean, we saw another car parked in the small car park. Its driver, who had been gently dozing, got out and introduced himself, as if this had been a meeting destined to be.

And indeed it was.

Meeting galactic astrologer Ray Mardyke by the light of the Full Moon, we were again reminded that nothing happens by chance.

Ray works with the archetypal energies of constellations rather than with the planetary alignments familiar to most astrologers. When we invited him to share a meal with us the following evening, I asked him whether he could shed any light on the turning of the 13th master key.

He didn't hesitate. 'Yes,' he replied.

Over dinner Ray explained that while most astrologers work with the familiar 12 zodiac signs, there is a 13th sign – that of Ophiuchus, the cosmic healer. Also associated with Asclepius, the Greek god of healing, it is portrayed as a man holding two great serpents. This star formation has also been interpreted as the embodiment of the Adam Kadmon, the perfected human of the Qabalah, with the serpents energetically representing our *kundalini* energy and symbolizing the transformation of our DNA.

The esoteric numerology of 13 is that of transformational wholeness – when we are able to embody unity consciousness in human form. This is revealed in a multitude of spiritual teachings and was embodied by Jesus with His 12 disciples and King Arthur with his 12 grail knights.

I was beginning to perceive the deeper significance of Ophiuchus when Ray then told us that the cosmic healer's foot was conjunct the centre of our Galaxy – symbolically and energetically stepping into the manifestation of such unity awareness. As I heard Ray's words, my galactic visions suddenly fell into place.

But more was revealed when we asked Ray about the significance of the date of 23 December 2003. He explained that each year the Sun traces a path through the sky against the backdrop of the constellations of the zodiac. Rising each day a little further along an arc, it creates a wave-like path north and south of the equator. In the northern hemisphere, the Sun's most northerly sunrise is at the winter solstice around 23 December. The relationship of the Earth to the constellations, however, undergoes a great cycle of nearly 26,000 years, caused by the Earth's wobble around its axis and known as 'the precession of the equinoxes'. Ray explained that it would only be in the year 2003, for the first time in that vast epoch, that the Sun would be positioned at this nexus of galactic alignment. Exactly on the December solstice, the Sun would be conjunct the foot of the constellation of Ophiuchus. As it reached that point, the Soular System would energetically unite through the embodiment of the galactic human with the galactic centre.

We at last began to understand why the Elohim had asked us to 'turn the 13th master key on 23 December 2003'. But it appeared that we were no closer to understanding the nature of the master key, why we'd been specifically guided to undertake this work at Avebury or the ultimate purpose of this culmination of our three-year odyssey.

*****

The geomantic energies of Kauai had felt profoundly nurturing and we had been held safe in their embrace from the moment we arrived. Maui was different.

Our short island-hopping flight had been uneventful until the plane began its descent and was caught by violent crosswinds. Everyone looked apprehensively at each other as the pilot skilfully guided us to a bumpy but safe landing. On the ground too, there was immediate chaos in organizing luggage and transport and we all felt uncomfortable and out of sorts. Eventually we arrived at the lovely house where we would be staying, but here too, despite its spectacular location overlooking the ocean, it just didn't feel right. Each of us reacted in a different way, either becoming annoyed and arguing with the situation or withdrawing in silence and refusing to engage.

Initially confused by the dramatic change of mood, I suddenly had a sense that geomantically the spirit of Maui was interacting with us as though he were a trickster. If this were a human relationship, we would stand up to him or withdraw, depending on our temperament. But a third option was to agree to dance with him, meeting and matching his mischievousness and sense of fun. When we became aware of this option and acted on it by regaining our own sense of humour, the energies suddenly shifted and the next morning we all felt welcomed and at ease.

Only later that day did we learn that the demi-god Maui, after whom the island was named, was indeed depicted as a trickster imbued with Herculean strength. It was Maui, according to legend, who had originally hauled the Hawaiian Islands from the depths of the ocean with a fishhook, and who had lassoed the Sun, refusing to release it until the islands were rescued from their ancient darkness and perpetually bathed in light.

From now on Maui was to be our friend and guide, as we continued to dance with him.

*****

In Alaska we had heard from Larry Merculieff about the Native American tradition of the male opening the portal for the female to do her healing work. Now in Hawaii, Ray had opened the door to a deeper understanding of these healing journeys.

In addition to his other revelations, he had also shed light on why the Elohim had guided us to go to Kauai first, before journeying on to Maui to activate the Soular Disc on 21 June at Haleakalā.

Laying out a map of the Hawaiian Islands for us, he had showed a straight alignment of volcanoes stretching from Kauai in the north-west through the islands of Oahu and Molokai to Haleakalā in the south-east and once more energetically embodying the elements of Fire and Water. It should have come as no surprise when he then told us that this line was also a solsticial marker. Sunrise at the winter solstice anchored the south-eastern end of the alignment and sunset at the summer solstice on 21 June anchored the north-western end over Kauai.

The direction of the alignment from north-west to south-east also explained why I'd been guided that we should activate the Haleakala Disc at sunset and not be there at sunrise – the usual time visitors to the volcano chose to experience this natural wonder. For the Sun, as seen from Haleakala, sets precisely over Kauai on 21 June – the day of greatest sunlight in the year.

Everything was rapidly falling into place and I could now see why we had been guided to visit Kauai first and could appreciate the perfection of the timing of our entire journey to Hawaii. By first connecting with the Earth-keeper crystal and then activating the Soular Disc, we would ensure that its energies, focused by the solsticial alignment, would open the door for the crystal and the female essence of Kauai to do their planetary work in preparation for the opening of a galactic portal.

*****

But before the activation, we had a few days to enjoy exploring Maui. Nowhere on Earth, it seemed, was the ease of being in the now, the gift of the present, more supported than on these islands.

Each day, as we drove to and from the light-filled house we now called home, we passed windsurfers skimming lightly over the water like dragonflies. Stopping to admire their grace and agility, I realized that surfing is a perfect metaphor for being in the now. To ride each wave requires an exquisite awareness of its timing – a willingness to join it as it rises, to be fully present through its strengthening and peaking, to accept letting go as it inevitably falls away and then to be centred in the moment until the next wave begins its flow. Any loss of presence, or of balance in riding the wave, and the surfer crashes into the chaos of foam and roiling water.

Some years ago, research showed that on average we spend around a third of our waking hours considering or thinking about the future – planning, projecting, dreaming or worrying. A further third or more of our time is taken up with thinking about the past – recalling its memories, being nostalgic for its good times or regretting those remembered as bad. When we are in the 'now', we are surfing the waves of time. Living in the past or the future, we either miss the wave or fall from it before it has completed its cycle.

It is in the now, and only in the now, that we can make our choices. It is only in the now that we can realize the ultimate reality of our being.

The nurturing breath of *aloha* lives in the eternal now. It is no surprise then, that the Hawaiian language only has a present tense.

*****

Legend tells that very early one morning Maui awoke and crept stealthily to the highest volcanic summit of his island. There he waited until the Sun rose and as each ray shone into the crater, he lassoed it and tied it to a *wiliwili* tree. The Sun begged for its freedom, but Maui refused until he had gained a promise to slow down its headlong flight across the sky each day.

To this day, the volcano is known as Haleakalā, 'the House of the Sun'. Its volcanic crater is massive – seven-and-a-half miles across and 3,000 feet deep. Born within the ocean depths, its rim is now over 10,000 feet above the waves and the mountain descends a further 19,000 feet to the ocean floor.

Tony and I awoke early on the morning of the solstice and stood together, silently greeting the Sun as it rose above the ocean horizon. I remembered that six years before, on the same day, I'd walked around Avebury henge with Wendy and Marko, her friend from Maui. We'd then shared a vision to celebrate rainbow bridge ceremonies at this ancient sacred place at each solstice. We had intuitively felt the call for people to come together at this time of greatest light to pray with others around the world for the healing of humanity's separation from itself and all life.

Now, six years and half a world away, I could never have consciously planned the perfection that Wendy and I and our fellow travellers would again be joined by Marko, who now lives on the slopes of Haleakalā, for this special day.

*****

The road to the summit of the ancient volcano snaked back and forth, climbing the 10,000 feet from the plain far below. We passed through cloud and came out into the bright sunshine of a glorious day.

Maui also brought us the joy of meeting up with astrologer Johnny Mirehiel and his partner Jan, who were to join us here in the activation of the Soular Disc. It had been Johnny who had discovered the astrological alignment and significance of the Harmonic Concordance that was to take place the coming November – the time when the Elohim had guided us to activate the 12th Soular Disc.

Standing on the vast crater rim of this House of the Sun, we felt as if we were on top of the world. Looking down over 3,000 feet into this immense grail, our breath was almost taken away by the spectacular sight of myriad minerals swirling in the frozen lava and creating a kaleidoscope of colours, ever-changing in the sunlight and fleeting cloud shadow.

The presence of the volcano-goddess Pele is powerful here. Many features within the crater relate to stories of her passing, and her artistic talents are noted in the area known as Pele's Paint-pot, due to the vibrant colours of its mineral deposits.

Just off the path, where we would tread lightly, Marko guided us to the summit of one of the many smaller volcanic cones dotted throughout the crater. Here in this place of natural sanctity we cleared a small space on the bare rock to make our simple altar and asked for the blessing of Maui, Pele and Haleakala itself for our healing work throughout this day and the activation of the Soular Disc energies at sunset.

The climb back up to the rim was a challenge for most of us in the hot sunshine, being further than we'd anticipated. Our friend Maui supported and energized those who needed his help.

Later, as the Sun began to sink in the sky behind Kauai far to the north-west, other local friends joined us at the Pu'u 'Ula'Ula lookout point on the summit of Haleakala. We formed a circle and shared the story of the Soular Discs. Saying our names, we created and focused our intention to be a collective physical and spiritual conduit to activate this 10th Disc.

I felt the benign presences of Pele and Maui join us to activate the energies of the Disc as with the last rays of the Sun the volcanic alignment was galvanized and the portal for Kauai to be empowered in her planetary work was opened.

Earlier, I'd left the pebble I'd brought from Easter Island at the heart of Haleakala's crater. As I did so, I felt strongly that we would need to activate the Disc and ask for Pele's and Maui's permission before taking a pebble from the volcano on to the next Disc.

Now, after the activation, with night rapidly falling I asked for their blessing and, sensing their positive response, found myself picking up two small pebbles of volcanic rock. Visitors to Hawaii are warned that taking such stones brings adversity and in many instances have posted them back to the islands when the warnings have come true! I knew, however, that with Pele's and Maui's blessings and their understanding that the pebbles were only taken in service to the highest purpose and not as a personal souvenir, I would be held safe.

*****

The next morning was cloudy. But when the rain came it passed quickly, leaving behind a miracle of light and a symbol of hope. It was unlike any rainbow any of us had ever experienced. Like a beautiful multi-hued ribbon, it appeared to lie only feet above the ground. As we watched, it began to arc upwards, as though raising itself, becoming ever brighter as it did so.

We stopped, as did others, not quite believing what we were seeing, open-mouthed with wonder. The arch felt like a portal into a new dimension of joy. And we thanked Maui for his abundance.

Our journey had begun with a sense of purpose anchored in the healing of relationships. In the dance of Kauai and Maui, we had learned new ways of being lovingly true to ourselves and to each other. Tony and I had felt all the residual pain from our Lemurian life almost effortlessly fall away, as though we had been destined to return to this place at this time to complete this purpose.

Our last day embodied this in a poignant way when we met Sunni, a Maui midwife who over the last 20 years has reintro-duced the birthing of infants in the ancient Hawaiian ways. Sunni's wisdom enables children to be born in water and at night by the natural and gentle light of the Moon and stars, without stress for mother or child. Incredible photographs of such a birth are suffused with light, and the auras of parents and child can be seen clearly.

Our experience of relationships begins with our birth. This is so often fraught emotionally and physically. Its common trauma of separation into an often harshly lit and alien environment may subsequently be held at a deep cellular level. In sacred pools such as those created by Sunni, often birthed at night by the soft natural light of the Moon, we can be born or reborn into a new way of being in relationship. Children delivered in this way are happier and gentler and enjoy a harmonious and joyous relation-ship with their parents and the world around them.

As I held *Sacred Birthing*, the book in which Sunni shares this wisdom, I burst into tears as I felt its love. Without needing to read a word, I knew it was a gift for the healing of humanity.

*****

The day before we were to say farewell to Hawaii, Tony had explored the path below our clifftop home and discovered a pool that we were told had been sacred to the ancient Hawaiians. Now, in the final hours before leaving, he led me there.

The pool lay silent and deep, cupped in the embrace of the cliff and facing the ocean. A waterfall flowed from the face of the cliff, energizing the pool and gently rippling its surface before spilling out over a flat rock to continue its journey to the sea.

We both knew this to be the place of our rebirth and our rededication to each other. Our ancient connections with Lemuria felt resolved and healed as, naked as children, we slipped into the water and allowed it to wash away all that no longer served us or supported our serving of others.

And as we climbed back up the cliff, we now felt strengthened to take our journeys with the Soular Discs to their completion.

*****

In Hawaii we had also begun to access directly the energies of the 11th chakra, which we were experiencing about 18 inches above our heads. We were beginning to realize that its energies were those of galactic awareness.

As an innate aspect of the wholeness of who we really are, it is the way-shower of our cosmic destiny.

🧩 🧩 🧩

CHAPTER 11
Reunion

CHAPTER 11

REUNION

September 2003

After the galactic insights of Hawaii, we returned home and I came back to Earth with a thud. While I usually enjoy the small pleasures and ordinary routine of my daily life, now the sense of deep connection I'd felt in Hawaii gave way to feelings of dislocation and exclusion. And I was unable to hear the guidance of the Elohim regarding the activation of the 11th Soular Disc.

Although I knew that the Disc was located somewhere in the southern Indian Ocean and had organized a journey to Madagascar to connect with it, over the last few weeks I had a growing sense that the journey would not go ahead. For by the time we'd left for Hawaii, only two people had expressed an interest in journeying with us to Madagascar. Unlike Chile and Easter Island, when I knew I had to go regardless, this felt different – without my understanding why.

*****

In Hawaii, I had been able to put all these concerns out of my mind while we focused on the activation of the 10th Disc. Now, back home, I had hoped to turn my attention to the 11th Disc.

The Elohim had guided me some time ago that its activation should take place on 11 September 2003, the second anniversary of the events of 9/11. In the inescapable horror of two years before, I had felt that in the collective crucible of this defining moment we were being offered a profound choice: to continue the separation within the world family or to begin to make choices based on love rather than fear. I sensed then that this was a threshold beyond which we were no longer able to energetically 'sit on the fence'.

Two years on, I felt the polarization or reunion of our choices and their implications becoming ever more stark. The healing activation of the 11th Disc seemed to offer the opportunity of reunion – to perceive and authentically begin to experience ourselves as a single human family and to find ways, however difficult and challenging, to come together.

I was also increasingly aware of the imminence of the Harmonic Concordance of early November, which would coincide with the activation of the 12th and final Soular Disc. This astrological alignment would form a perfect six-pointed Star in the sky. Each of the six planets exquisitely forming the points of the Star would harmoniously interact to support the overall essence of this cosmic mandala which was seen as presaging the personal embodiment of unity awareness.

A total lunar eclipse lay at the heart of the alignment. The Sun at the apex of a trinity of planets would influence Saturn and Mars. The Moon would be opposite the Sun at the apex of a second interconnecting trinity with Jupiter and Chiron, the wounded healer.

The Sun in the zodiac sign of Scorpio during the alignment would reflect the need to 'die' to old ways of being in order to be 'reborn'. Mars in the sign of Pisces would offer the passion for surrender and union with the divine, while Saturn in Cancer would support the discipline to do what was ultimately life-sustaining.

The second trinity of this hugely significant alignment had the Moon in Taurus emphasizing the fecundity of the Earth as a source of our nurturing and conjunct with the soul's purpose. Jupiter would be in Virgo, aligned to support the spiritual goals and philosophy needed to purify and create the optimal circumstances to birth the soul-awakened human. Finally, Chiron positioned in Capricorn would facilitate the healing of our deepest wounds relating to our heritage.

We would activate the 12th Soular Disc and in doing so complete that of the unity grid of Gaia at the timing of the Harmonic Concordance in the early hours of universal time of 9 November 2003. And thus the 9/11 activation of the 11th Disc would mirror and further energize the 11/9 timing of the 12th and the completion of the work that Tony and I had begun 39,000 years ago.

*****

But as time passed and the day of the activation rapidly approached, the likelihood of journeying to the Indian Ocean was equally rapidly receding.

I reached out to the Elohim once more, asking for their guidance. This time I heard them and finally I understood. They explained that until now, each Disc had required a physical human presence in order to anchor our intention and enable its activation. Even the Antarctica Disc had required the earlier physical connection with Anita to enable us to co-create an energetic bridge to it from Santiago. Only in Hawaii had our combined intention become sufficiently empowered to no longer need our physical connection for the 11th Disc.

This not only explained why we didn't need to physically journey to it but also why my guidance couldn't be clarified until after the activation of the Soular Disc in Hawaii.

But a further surprise awaited me.

The Elohim had guided that the 11th Disc was located in the southern Indian Ocean. I'd assumed when looking at the map that the island of Madagascar was the closest land and so had planned the original journey there. Now, realizing that we could activate the Disc from a distance, I was also inspired to go back to the map. When I did, only a few days before the activation was due to take place, I suddenly understood why.

There, in the midst of the huge expanse of the Indian Ocean, was a tiny island called Reunion. And I realized that the centre of the Disc's energies was *here*.

*****

I was still feeling dislocated, as though my inner being was at war with itself, when with only three days to go before the 11 September activation I woke from a vivid dream:

> It was a bright sunlit day and I was standing in an enormous open yard. In the distance were drab institutional buildings and a couple of high towers and I realized that I was in a huge prison compound. My attention, though, was focused on the people who were milling about in the yard.
>
> As I walked forward, I saw that they were fighting each other in a chaotic mêlée.
>
> I somehow knew that it was no use asking them what they were fighting about, but I nonetheless perceived that my purpose was to help them find a peaceful way forward.
>
> I realized that however loudly I shouted, they wouldn't be able to hear me. But I understood that without raising my voice I could reach into their hearts. Quietly, I asked them to choose representatives to talk to each other in an attempt to resolve their differences.
>
> Despite the uproar of the fight, there was a sudden silence as they heard my heart-centred request and turned to face me.

As a few of their number stepped forward and began to walk towards me, I had a fleeting sense that they had already made their choice for peace.

Still processing the import of the dream, but now feeling better than I had for weeks, I wasn't able to share it with Tony before he left for work. Arriving home that evening, he told me that he'd managed to research Reunion in our local library.

This is what he discovered: Centuries ago this tiny island was a place of outcasts, pirates, slavers and slaves. It was infamous – the entire island was a prison colony for those who had been judged and excluded. Life there was harsh, violence was rife and survival tenuous, even for the strongest.

Against all the odds, at some point the people of Reunion stopped judging themselves and others and made choices of love. And now the island is a peaceful, vibrant and multi-ethnic society, a microcosm of the possibilities for a wider world.

This was my dream real-ized and my inner turmoil healed!

*****

Corresponding to the time that the first plane had hit the twin towers in New York two years before, we now invited each of those who were journeying with us in Spirit to add their unique voice to a global prayer for Reunion – within themselves, within our collective human family and within the matrix of life that is our Soular System. We invited everyone, in whatever way they felt guided and for however long, to focus their intention and awareness on the reality of reunion in heart, mind and spirit, so that we might celebrate all that we were in peace, joy and wholeness.

A few of us had arranged to meet in the heart of the Avebury landscape for the activation of the Reunion Disc. In the gentle rain of a grey day, we walked together up to one of the most ancient monuments in this sacred land, overlooking Silbury Hill and the place of the Soular Disc crop circle of five years before.

Walking this sacred land again and knowing that this would be where, in a further two months, we would activate the 12th Disc at Silbury Hill, I felt a profound sense of reunion and impending homecoming.

Some people who had intended to physically be with us were unexpectedly caught up in traffic and so connected energetically instead. And so, as the rain continued to fall, we were six.

Standing within the womb-like chamber of the ancient long barrow, mentored by its aetheric guardian, we attuned together and focused our intention on a sense of compassionate reunion. I felt deep within myself the re-soulution of ancient separations and powerfully felt the activation of the Disc many thousands of miles away.

Suddenly the six-pointed star of the Harmonic Concordance astrological alignment shone brightly in my inner vision.

As we smiled at each other, we realized that all of us had sensed the activation of the Disc and knew that the empowerment of our collective co-creation was indeed strengthening.

Placing the two pebbles from Haleakalā within the ancient sanctity of the long barrow, I suddenly understood that the six of us here formed the geomantic rainbow bridge to a 12th activation and the culmination of the Harmonic Concordance.

And as we came out into the light of day, the mist cleared and the Sun began to shine.

*****

In the 18th century, the English mystic and visionary William Blake foresaw the symbolic rebuilding of the holy city of Jerusalem in the land he called Albion. This was the ancient mystical name for England, the White Land, so called because at its heart was the pure white chalk landscape of Avebury and Stonehenge.

The term 'Albion' also refers to the mythic landscape giant which Blake perceived as being held captive by an enchantment woven by the petty politics and prejudicial moralities of his day. Like others before him, he prophesied an end to the wasteland and a spiritual resurrection arising from the reconciliation of all the people of Albion.

Our final pilgrimage would be through the land of Albion. The culmination of our long journey was now only a few short weeks away.

❄ ❄ ❄

CHAPTER 12

Albion

ALBION

November 2003

It was master geomancer John Michell who first identified a landscape alignment of natural and monumentalized sacred places dedicated to the archangel St Michael extending through Albion from the extreme south-west of Cornwall in a north-easterly direction to the coast of East Anglia. It follows the longest continuous stretch of land in southern England, with Avebury and Silbury Hill positioned at its *omphalos,* or energetic centre-point.

John named the line after St Michael as so many hills and churches directly on its path are dedicated to the Archangel, whom many mystics perceive as a spiritual leader of this epochal shift of consciousness of Gaia and all her children. The associations of St Michael with dragons also suggested that the line marked a telluric energy current or dragon path.

When dowser Hamish Miller and researcher Paul Broadhurst then dowsed the alignment, they confirmed John's intuition and discovered it to be a yang or 'male' energy current. Continuing to plot its naturally sinuous path as far as Avebury, they realized that here it is partnered with a yin or 'female' telluric energy current. This they named the Mary line, after noting its many associations with holy springs and wells dedicated to St Mary. At places such as Glastonbury Tor and Avebury, they found that these two complementary currents conjoin in a sacred and powerful telluric marriage.

The caduceus formed by the Michael and Mary dragon paths curves around the 'staff' of the St Michael alignment. And thus the landscape of Albion embodies the geomantic symbol of the healer Asclepius, which, as we had discovered, is represented by the 13th zodiac sign – the galactic constellation of Ophiuchus.

*****

Our journey through Albion would dance with the Michael and Mary energy lines from the Isles of Scilly in the far south-west through Cornwall and on to Glastonbury and Avebury, culminating with the activation of the Soular Disc at Silbury Hill at the time of the Harmonic Concordance – in accordance with the guidance of the Elohim.

Journeying with the Soular Discs over the last three years, our understanding of the significance of '12 around 1' as the physical embodiment of christed or unity consciousness continued to deepen.

The cosmic archetypes of the zodiac combine with the biblical archetypes of Jesus and His disciples. In Albion, the enduring archetypal mythos which permeates this land is that of King Arthur and his knights. Here too the solar – or soular – hero is surrounded by 12 companions. Ultimately, the 12 and the 1 culminate to form a 13th transformative whole.

In essence, both the Master Jesus and Arthur only embody the entirety of their soular 'kingship' when they symbolically integrate the consciousness of the aspects of their 12 disciples or knights too.

As we ultimately heal into the wholeness of who we really are, we also progressively embody the experience of these 12 aspects of our cosmic consciousness, together forming the 13th awareness and embodiment of unity – the All-Oneness of the Cosmos.

*****

Our final pilgrimage, lasting 13 days, began appropriately at Tintagel, the legendary birthplace of King Arthur.

This rocky headland on the northern coast of Cornwall is beautiful in summer and bleak in winter. Continually pounded by the Atlantic waves, it stands adamant, the guardian of profound knowledge of the essence of the land and its people. A nexus of telluric energies and leys, it anchors a winter-solstice solar alignment with Stowe's Hill in the centre of Cornwall. In Old English *stowe* means 'sacred place' and here the Michael and Mary caduceus meets at a node point. It is fitting that the enduring mythos of Arthur, this solar/soular hero, begins here.

Legend tells that Arthur's father, King Uther Pendragon, fell in love with Ygraine, Duchess of Cornwall, who was already married to Uther's liegeman, Duke Gorlois. Unable to restrain his passion, Uther asked his advisor, the great magician and sage Merlyn, to help him win Ygraine. Merlyn agreed, but with one proviso – that any child born of their union would be his to guard and guide.

Luring Gorlois away from his windswept castle at Tintagel, Merlyn glamoured Uther to look like his rival. Gaining access to Ygraine's chamber, Uther slept with the unsuspecting duchess and Arthur was conceived.

The following day, Gorlois died in the fierce fighting against his and Uther's common enemy and Uther, now known to Ygraine, was free to marry her.

And so it was that Arthur, the great hero of Albion, was conceived in deceit and betrayal.

*****

On a warm and windswept day, we stood on the cliffs of the mainland and looked across to Tintagel. Naturally sculpted by wind and sea, the profile of a rugged face is clearly etched in the cliff face, offering a beguiling focus for our connection with Arthur and his mythic role in the story of Albion.

Thinking of the circumstances of his conception, I mulled over how often we have been told, or indeed tell ourselves, that 'the end justifies the means'. I knew now that for our inner healing, such deception only holds us in the old patterns of separation. For inevitably the means *become* the end

On our continuing journey of healing, it felt appropriate that here, at the birthplace of Arthur, we should pray for loving truth to be reborn.

Exploring the mainland clifftop overlooking Tintagel, Brian had been drawn to a slab of stone which he'd called 'the king seat'. His attunement had recognized that it gave access to an aetheric chamber within the cliff, but also that he, sensing his embodiment of the archetype of Merlyn during this journey, was not to enter.

Without being told by Brian what to expect, I sat down on the king seat. Suddenly I found myself in a small chamber with shimmering crystalline walls. The cave wall facing the sea then gently dissolved and I looked out onto the vastness of the ocean.

I felt a familiar presence and recognized Merlyn, who gently placed an unadorned circlet of gold around my brow. I knew that for this journey I was now to embody the archetypal energy of Arthur and the return of 'the once and future king'.

The essence of Merlyn, the wisdom keeper of the Arthurian mythos, was to lightly guide our steps through this land of magic and transformation. His archetypal energies have often been associated with Thoth, the Egyptian god of wisdom and our guide from our first Soular Disc journey three years before. I felt deeply grateful that in his aspect of Merlyn he now guided our homecoming.

*****

A few miles north of Tintagel, running inland from the coastal road, is the magical St Nectan's glen, whose wooded valley is a tranquil sanctuary for the devic and elementary realms of faerie.

In the dappled sunlight beneath the trees, we followed the narrow path alongside a bubbling stream, each one of us gradually falling into a silent reverie. With each step, as we moved further away from the busy road and deeper into the glen, the faerie energies became more abundant and empowered. This was their home and we were grateful visitors.

At the head of the glen and below the tiny stone chamber reputed to be the hermit's cell of St Nectan, a sparkling waterfall tumbles into a deep pool. Standing close to its rainbow spray, in the misted air, and looking at the clear pool alive with undines, we all felt the presence of these elemental beings of water.

As we journeyed on, the devic and elemental beings of Gaia continued to play shyly with us. The gnomic earth elementals, the sylphs of the air and the salamanders of fire all became our companions through this ancient and fey landscape. Sometimes sensing them subtly from a distance and at other times feeling them closely, we revelled in their presence.

*****

A day later, a tiny prop-engined plane carried us in two relays to the landing strip on St Mary's, the largest of the Isles of Scilly. These islands, seen by some students of the ancient ways as being the last vestiges of the fabled land of Lyonesse, are spoken of in the Arthurian legends as having been cataclysmically drowned. To some, they may even be the northern reaches of lost Atlantis. Given the rising sea levels since the last Ice Age, they may be indeed.

Here the remains of turf-covered barrows hold the ancient memory of the now drowned landscape, the concentration of these megalithic remains testifying to the significance of this land from earliest times. And as we walked in the unseasonable but welcome sunshine to these chambered cairns, we could hear the soft voices of the old ones speaking to us across the millennia.

They spoke of peaceful communities living in harmony with the land and the ocean. And here there was no echo of the many grievings we had shared elsewhere, only the quiet acknowledgement of the eternal cycles of birth and life and an honouring of the passing between realms.

Celtic lore talks of 'the Isles of the Blest' – the land to the west, where heroes and kings rest from their Earthly labours. We travellers too, nurtured in the late autumn warmth and in the blessed energies of St Mary's embrace, felt at peace.

All too soon, it was time for us to journey on, and back on the mainland we drove north to a meeting with dowsers Hamish and Ba Miller. Sharing the stories of our journeys, we laughed as we realized that their visits to South Africa and New Zealand had, over the last couple of years, also called them to the locations of the Soular Discs.

As we walked into their sitting room, Tony's eyes were drawn to a pile of books – Hamish's as yet unread pile – and especially the one on the top, *The Galaxy on Earth* by Richard Leviton.

As we busied ourselves with tea and Ba's delicious cakes, Tony handed me the book.

Opening it, my jaw dropped. For here, in perhaps the least expected place and in the most mundane way, two final and crucial pieces of the jigsaw were about to fall into place.

Richard is a geomancer who, like Tony and me, works geomythically with the Earth and the Cosmos. We understand and perceive the Cosmos as an interrelated conscious whole and encounter it at many levels of awareness. This includes our honouring of the messages of dreams and omens and communication with a multitude of discarnate beings.

Richard describes Albion as geomythically representing the entirety of the Galaxy expressed as a generic human figure and considers that this cosmic blueprint is imprinted at three holographic levels within the Earth's energy field.

The first level he perceives is through a complex interweaving of landscape zodiacs, each embodying the 12 into 13 harmonic. When a zodiac is activated by the co-creative co-operation of the elemental, human and angelic realms, its Albion energetically awakes.

The second level of the Albion imprint is at each of the 12 faces of the dodecahedral unity grid of the Earth, the etheric body of Gaia, which at its highest and most complete level, is also an Albion.

The third level of Albion, as understood by Richard, is embodied energetically by the entire planet, which, when fully integrated and thus activated, includes the awareness of the first and second levels.

This third and whole Albion represents and contains the totality of human conscious experience on the Earth from the beginning. In effect it is humanity's collective higher self – what we had progressively experienced throughout our global pilgrimage.

Reading Richard's words, I knew their truth from our direct experience at each step of our global journeying and I now felt we were truly coming home.

*****

While everyone was chatting and drinking tea, I sat quietly. While part of me remained anchored in the bustle of the room, I could feel the hologram of my awareness grow and grow and grow. Embodying a sense of the potential wholeness of my personal being, I expanded to integrate my being with that of the living Earth and beyond, encompassing the entirety of the consciousness of our Soular System.

In the midst of an 'ordinary' day, I felt the 'extraordinary' integration of the 12 chakras into the 13th wholeness of my unity energy field. I became the energetic embodiment of the landscape Albion we were integrating during this our 12th journey.

As I expanded my perception still further, I sensed the coming embodiment of the planetary Albion, soon to be activated. I now knew beyond doubt that the turning of the 13th master key would expand our consciousness still further and energetically manifest the Albion of our entire Soular System. And for the first time, I could sense the future opening of the portal enabling our physical embodiment of unity consciousness – birthing our cosmic destiny of becoming galactic humans.

Richard's insights also explained why 'turning the 13th master key' needed to take place at Avebury.

Avebury is in my heart, but when I'd received guidance from the Elohim to 'turn the 13th master key' there, I had been loath to emphasize its significance. The entire Earth to me is sacred – and I know a few people who maintain that their home is *the* most important place on the planet!

Until now, I hadn't been sure whether Avebury's relationship with the master key was unique or whether our work could also be accomplished elsewhere. Richard's perspective brought clarity, for he described Avebury's geomantic role as being unique in being the planetary umbilicus – the place where the Earth plugs into the centre of the Galaxy.

And now at last I understood the guidance of the Elohim, because it was only at Avebury, through its umbilical connection to the Galaxy, that the energetic resonance throughout the entire Albion hologram could be birthed.

Drinking tea in Hamish and Ba's sitting room and surrounded by the laughing voices of my friends, I felt that such revelations underlined yet again the dance of our ordinary and extraordinary experience.

*****

The trinity of Glastonbury, Stonehenge and Avebury has been called 'the Aquarian triangle' and our understanding of the significance of these three ancient icons of the new age is still unfolding.

Our onward journey now brought us first to Glastonbury, whose high Tor is believed by many who feel the call to settle here to be the legendary Isle of Avalon, the final resting-place of King Arthur. The archaeological discovery of the 'Sweet Track', a 6,000-year-old wooden causeway through the marshy land then surrounding the Tor and the stilt-built houses of the later lake villages, shows that millennia ago it was indeed an island.

Other archaeological finds have also evidenced that two millennia ago Glastonbury was a thriving community enjoying trade from as far afield as the eastern Mediterranean. But Glastonbury's true importance lies in the richness of its spiritual and geomythic heritage.

On the summit of the Tor, rising magically up from the surrounding Somerset Levels, stands the ruined tower of the ancient church dedicated to St Michael. The Michael and Mary caduceus weaving around its slopes meets at a node point on the high slope below the tower before journeying on.

Standing together on the summit, we felt the power of its ancient energies welling up here and of the vast landscape temple energetically embodied in this land of myth and revelation.

Nestled further below, on the lower slopes of the Tor, the peaceful gardens of Chalice Well are an oasis of nurturing and healing energy. The Red spring and the White spring, waters that have separately percolated through the rock for millennia absorbing the telluric power of the Tor, rise from its lower reaches and flow together through the Chalice Well gardens.

It is to somewhere nearby, held safe within the Tor, that the legends say the Holy Grail of the Last Supper of Jesus, which held His blood at His crucifixion, was brought.

And it is believed that for perhaps thousands of years an avenue of oak trees, revered by the Druidic geomancers of Celtic Albion and continually replanted with the acorns from ageing trees, wove its way down the Tor to a sacred grove. The devic tree spirits or dryads have continued to hold this place safe generation after generation until now, when only two ancient trees, Gog and Magog, remain.

As I stood on the Tor, looking out at the landscape, I thought of the work of the artist and mystic Katherine Maltwood, who had a revelatory vision of a 12-fold zodiac imprinted in the landscape around Glastonbury. In essence the zodiac that Maltwood called 'the Temple of the Stars' is a natural feature whose massive figures, shaped by hills and partially outlined by watercourses, depict a circular complex some 12 miles across. Yet in many places, irrigation channels and modern roads are incorporated into the figures, rendering the whole a partnership between Gaia and humankind.

For those who see the zodiac, it is physically real, as it was to us on that day. To others, it is an illusion, a huge landscape Rorschach test where we are asked to identify pattern and meaning in apparent randomness. I ruefully smiled to myself as I pondered on the mindset of Western culture and our collective choice over the last 300 years to see with materialistic eyes. We are unaccustomed to perceiving the deeper truths of the Cosmos as the ancients did and as the primary peoples of the Earth, such as the Australian Aborigines, still do. They see myth and legend and so experience it. They see magic and so experience it.

A new vision of integral reality is, however, emerging from the reconciliation of leading-edge science and perennial wisdom, as we are re-membering the wholeness of the world and our place within it. Our choices now are to remain within the self-limitations of a materialistic worldview or to be open to the possibilities of a conscious Cosmos with we ourselves as co-creators.

As we followed the path down the Tor, my thoughts drifted back over our journeys and our encounters with primary peoples, perhaps our greatest living teachers of how to balance such greater awareness while still honouring our Earth walk as human beings. More than ever, I now appreciated the extraordinary awareness that is available to us as we re-member our spiritual wholeness and the ordinary miracle of our expressing all that we are through our human experience. And again I gave thanks to the Elohim and all those who have been our way-showers on our journey home.

*****

The Arthurian mythos is also directly embodied in Glastonbury's long history. Legend tells that after his last battle, the mortally wounded Arthur was carried to the Isle of Avalon to rest and sleep until a time when he would be needed to save the land of Albion once more.

Many speak of Glastonbury as the fabled Avalon. Indeed, the bodies of a 'tall man and a golden-haired woman' said to be those of Arthur and his Queen Guenevere are reputed to have been discovered buried in the grounds of Glastonbury Abbey in medieval times by the monks. While the remains and a lead cross within the grave naming them were lost in the religious turmoil of the sixteenth century, the legend endures.

Even if only symbolically, the association of Arthur – the solar/soular hero – with Glastonbury is in harmony with the most significant of all the attributes of this place.

The legend that Joseph of Arimathea founded the first Christian church in Albion here, carrying the Grail and bringing the unconditionally loving teachings of Jesus to this place, also continues to endure.

Even more powerful is the legend that Jesus himself walked the land of Albion, as William Blake in his poem 'Jerusalem' asks:

And did those feet in ancient times walk upon England's mountains green?
And was the holy lamb of God on England's pleasant pastures seen?

Between the ages of 12, when He was presented to the priests in the temple at Jerusalem, and the beginning of His ministry at the age of 30, the Bible is completely silent on the life of Jesus. Is it possible that, as the legends say, in His youth He came to Albion with Joseph, who was purported to be His uncle, and even perhaps later as a young adult?

But why would Jesus and Joseph have come here? The prosaic view is that Joseph may have traded in the locally mined metals and that business may have brought him to Glastonbury, bringing Jesus with him. But could there have been a more profound reason for their visit? Is it possible that they came to meet the leaders of the old religion of the Celtic Druids, the descendants of the master geomancers who constructed Stonehenge and Avebury millennia before?

Centuries before Jesus may have walked the hills and vales of Albion, the Greek philosopher and geometer Pythagoras spent much of his life learning the wisdom traditions of other countries. A number of contemporary and later writers noted that he was instructed in the teachings of the Druids, who were renowned for their deep insights into the nature of the Cosmos, in common with the other perennial wisdom of the ancient world.

The esoteric teachings of the Hebraic Essenes, the likely tradition into which Jesus was born, and those of the earliest Christianity suggest that they too shared this knowledge. Indeed, what little we know of the traditions of the Druids and the remarkable way in which they peacefully gave way to early Christian influences strongly suggests that their own teachings were predisposed to those of the Master Jesus and that all were elements in an ancient tapestry of profound wisdom which is now reawakening.

*****

Our next destination was one of the icons of this ancient tradition and the second apex of the Aquarian triangle – Stonehenge.

To walk between the great sarsen stone portals of Stonehenge at any time of the day is a memorable experience. To be held within the embrace of the stone guardians at dawn is unforgettable.

The discovery of post-holes which once held massive wooden poles has shown that this temple of the Cosmos and its environs have been sacred for at least 10,000 years. The monument we experience today, however, is the last stage in an evolutionary process that began over five millennia ago.

Stonehenge includes alignments to both the Sun and Moon, and the yearly cycle of the Earth with the Sun, which resonates in a 12-fold harmonic, and that of the Earth with the Moon, which resonates in a 13-fold pattern of 'moonths', are embodied in the space-time metrology of this cosmic temple.

As the Sun rose on the morning of our visit, we asked for the blessing of the aetheric guardian of this place of power and, individually and together, attuned to the profound wisdom resonating in the crystalline matrix of its massive sarsen stone circle.

Many years ago, when I began to visit Stonehenge regularly, I became able to connect energetically with its guardian. One morning, as I asked his blessing to enter within the stones, he said, 'Look at the faces.'

He guided me to walk around the outside of the monument, and as I did so, I clearly saw a face in each of the great sarsens, looking out from the stone as if protecting this ancient temple. As I acknowledged each one, the guardian told me that these were the faces of the ancient priests who had chosen, as he had himself, to remain here to guard this sacred place.

Over the years, they have all become my friends.

*****

Travelling the short distance from Stonehenge to Avebury, we came home to our final destination – the third and final apex of the Aquarian Triangle.

The Avebury area has, like Stonehenge, been a place of significance from the earliest times for the peoples who walked lightly on this land. Some six millennia ago, they began to create enduring monuments of stone here – they began to alter the Earth. Over millennia, they continued to harmonize the sacred landscape through immense communal effort, cosmologically idealizing the Avebury environs as the microcosm of a perceived macrocosmic order.

Exquisitely, the monuments here incorporate this ancient geomantic wisdom. As the Michael and Mary energies dance through Avebury's sacred precincts, they come together in a trinity of node points within what 18th-century antiquarian William Stukeley called 'the serpent temple'.

At the heart of the Avebury sacred landscape are the two monuments that embody the essence of its purpose – the great henge of Avebury and the majestic Silbury Hill.

At Avebury we'd planned to meet the remaining members of our group who would be with us for the last few days of our journey. We had been 11 during our Albion pilgrimage so far and would be 14 for the completion of our journey and activation of the 12th Soular Disc. While 14 is a perfectly acceptable number, I had a nagging sense that we should be 13, physically embodying the transformative wholeness that our journeys had progressively revealed.

As we were travelling the final few miles to Avebury, we received a message. One of those who had planned to be with us was unable to make it. As we called to commiserate with her and send her our love and best wishes, I suddenly appreciated that we were to be 13 after all.

I knew that we were now ready to anchor the transformational energies of the coming days.

It now really began to feel that all the threads of our multi-dimensional journeys were finally being woven into a tapestry of awareness whose form was becoming clear and ever more whole.

The reality of completing the 12 activations at the time of the Harmonic Concordance was very near. Over the last few weeks I'd become ever more aware of the questions of those around me – and my own. What would occur, on both energetic and physical levels, and what would 'afterwards' be like?

I didn't know.

All I did know was that whatever happened, my inexorable choice was to embody the understanding of love that the journeys had taught me – and the hope that 'afterwards' still included chocolate biscuits and red wine!

*****

Finally, 8 November dawned.

We 13 travellers made ready to meet the larger group who would join us for the day in the Avebury landscape and then the much larger gathering for the ceremonies to activate the Soular Disc and to celebrate the Harmonic Concordance.

We shared our understanding of what was unfolding and the significance of this sacred landscape as we walked around the ancient stone circle of Avebury henge.

Many geomancers have perceived Avebury henge as representing an energetic and symbolic *omphalos,* or navel. Lying in a landscape bowl and surrounded by a high bank and a deep inner ditch, it is essentially a hidden world. Entering through one of the four causeways cut into its bank, with its ditch, once twice as deep as it is now, falling away on either side, one experiences what it is to feel at the centre of the world – the *axis mundi* of existence.

Four thousand or more years ago, one would have walked between massive portals of stone into the interior of this great amphitheatre and geomantic wonder of the world.

From his dowsing, Hamish Miller had perceived the primary elemental attributes of the Michael and Mary telluric currents as being of Fire and Water – which, as we had discovered, was also the elemental essence of the Soular Discs.

In 1988, at Beltane, traditionally the early May festival of the sacred marriage at human and telluric levels, Hamish had also discovered a new patterning at the Michael and Mary node point within the Avebury henge. A nested trinity of 12-pointed stars had emerged centred there. Later, checking other nodes, he discovered that they too now incorporated this geomantic pattern. Did this embodiment of the trinity and the 12-fold harmonic presage the geomantic awakening whose birth was now imminent?

As we now walked this landscape, so familiar and beloved, I also knew there was a deeper level of awareness now ready to emerge. I began to feel the stirrings of a third energy current within the land, interwoven with the Michael and Mary energies and embodying the essence of the cosmic child – the co-creative force of the Cosmos.

*****

We now knew that the activation of the Soular Disc at Silbury Hill at the time of the Harmonic Concordance would complete the activation of the unity grid of Gaia – in geomancer Richard Leviton's words, 'awaken the 12 chakras of the planetary Albions'.

And offer us the opportunity to make our individual choices to embody unity consciousness within ourselves.

*****

The Elohim had guided us to offer a trinity of ceremonies:

- The first, at sunset on 8 November, was to honour and to release any and all old patterns of separation.

- The second, at the time of the Harmonic Concordance in the early hours of 9 November, was to activate the ascended consciousness of individuals through the energies of the Harmonic Concordance and to communally activate the final Soular Disc and thus the entire Albion of Gaia.
- The third ceremony, at dawn on the same day, was to celebrate a new beginning.

As sunset approached, more and more people began to arrive at the seed-point of the journeys where the Soular Disc crop circle had been five years before. Guarded by the West Kennet long barrow to the south and with Silbury Hill prominent to the north, we began the first ceremony.

To energetically release the old patterns of separation and limiting fears, we invited everyone present to write their intentions of letting go and healing on a slip of paper. As they were doing so, we lit a fire for them to then consign their intentions to the flames. For over an hour, each person in turn came forward, the only sound in the still night air being the pure and gentle tone of my ancient Tibetan bowl attuned to the heart.

When everyone had enacted their intention and completed their inner work, in the darkness before Moonrise we said our farewells until later, when we would return for the time of the Harmonic Concordance ceremony and the activation of the 12th Soular Disc.

At midnight we joined many others to form a great circle around a central fire – much appreciated on this cold night. The sky was cloud-filled and the Full Moon hidden from our sight. Now we were higher up the slope of the hillside and nearer the long barrow. I could barely make out Silbury Hill, but I could powerfully feel its energetic presence and had a sense of expectation as the time for the activation of the Disc drew near.

Once everyone was made welcome, the ceremony began by inviting 12 of the Soular Disc travellers to express their feelings about the essence of the healing they had experienced. Each in turn stepped forward into the circle and spoke movingly of the awareness they had gained over the last three years. For each of the 12 journeys, one of the travellers described the culmination of our collective understanding:

- Brian explained how in Egypt, in learning to take responsibility for our own choices we had come to embrace the light and shadow within others and integrate it within ourselves.
- Derriel spoke of how in South Africa we had learned to celebrate rather than fear diversity and to recognize the underlying unity of all life.
- Rona described how China had offered us the opportunity to transcend our judgement of others and ourselves and to begin to re-member and reconcile our extraterrestrial heritage.
- Emma shared how Alaska had gifted us the understanding that it is only by being willing to let go and grieve that ultimate reconciliation is possible.
- Melinda spoke of how Peru had taught us the lesson of being able to be both visible and invisible, embodying both visible empowerment and invisible service.
- Suzie explained that in Australia we had begun to experience healing at archetypal levels, feeling our connection with all life with empathy and understanding.
- And Mary revealed how, journeying on to New Zealand, we had appreciated the need to honour and not abuse the vulnerability of others and ourselves.
- The understanding gained in activating the Antarctic Soular Disc, as described by Jennifer, was for us to individually and collectively allow our ice-soulation to melt.
- Sharon spoke of how, on the tiny speck of land that is Easter Island, a microcosm of Gaia, we learned to hear our inner voice, to listen to it and to act upon it.
- I stepped forward to share how the *aloha* of Hawaii had

offered us the homecoming of being lovingly true in relationships.
- And then Annette spoke of how Reunion had showed us how
to embody our intention that each thought, word and action
would be a continuing prayer of reunion.
- Finally, at the culmination of our global odyssey here in
Albion, Tony spoke of how we had come to finally know our
wholeness with All Life.

While it remained unsaid, I knew too that at the heart of all our
journeys of inner transformation was a willingness to show up –
a courage to commit to the quest wherever it led.

By the light of the central fire, I could see those close to me
quietly nod and glance at each other as they recognized the
similarities between our inner journeys, our challenges and strug-
gles, and their own.

Just after 1 a.m., at the moment of the lunar eclipse, the planetary alignment of the Harmonic Concordance formed its exquisite pattern in the sky.

The six of us who had connected to the 11th Soular Disc now
walked forward, linking hands to mirror the alignment in microcosm.

A seventh joined us.

Justina had gifted the crucial insight that the planetary matrix
of the Concordance needed the involvement of the Earth to
ground its transformational energies. As she took her place,
embodying the Earth, at the centre of our microcosmic alignment, together with all those present, we attuned with highest
intention to its influence.

As I offered and supported our individual choices to become
whole and embody unity consciousness, I felt the energies of the
Concordance flowing gently and easily through me, and sensed
the seven of us energetically meld into one as we stood together
in our unity of purpose.

We returned to our places in the circle and now everyone, more than 150 people, took their turn in making their own individual choices out loud, co-creating, in the Now of this magnificent moment, a unified tapestry of empowered intention.

Deeply moved, I sat intently focusing on each person as they made their declaration.

Suddenly I heard a woman's voice cry, 'The Moon!' Sure enough, above us, the Full Moon peeped shyly from behind the cloud. The eclipse was almost complete. And I could feel the 12th Soular Disc and the entire unity grid of the Earth come to its final stage of activation as Gaia too made her choice.

*****

By the Moon's now radiant light the completion of our ceremony was to walk through this sacred landscape to geomantically ground the healing energies of this cosmic gift and the reawakening of the unity grid.

Tony led those who had chosen to walk the landscape while I, balancing the extraordinary with the ordinary once more, took those who needed some rest before the dawn ceremony back to their hotel.

Later, without sleep and bathed in the silvery light of the Moon, I waited for the walkers to return.

In those quiet hours of the night, I looked back over the incredible journey of the last three years and felt throughout my being how my own perception of the Cosmos had been transformed.

And knew that this was just the beginning.

Over those three years, the Albion of my own energy field had become activated through the portal of the 8th chakra of the universal heart. The earthstar chakra beneath my feet was continuing to reveal and deepen my connection with the multidimensional realms of Gaia. My early explorations through the 10th and 11th chakras were opening vast memories and future dreams of my relationships with All Life throughout our Soular System and our entire Galaxy.

And, like a child taking her first steps, I was beginning to journey beyond even the almost infinite reaches of the Cosmos to perceive and feel a sense of the unity consciousness that birthed and continues to co-create this everlastingly wondrous dance of awareness.

I smiled as through the darkness I glimpsed the first walkers returning and joined them as they completed their journey. And as dawn began to lighten the sky, we were all in a joyous mood for our celebration of rebirth.

Under a clear morning sky, we sang and drummed and danced.

*****

The unity grid of Gaia is now activated and the planetary Albion awakened.

Our individual choices, cosmically supported by the Harmonic Concordance, are also now readying our embodiment of the microcosmic Albion of our human experience.

We now understood why the turning of the 13th master key needed to be at Avebury on 23 December 2003.

And we realized that our work was to culminate at that moment in the opening of a portal for galactic consciousness to stream through the umbilical cord of Avebury and usher in the birth pangs of our cosmic destiny.

THE DAY OUT OF TIME
23 December 2003

The 23rd day of the 12th month of the year 2003 adds up to and embodies the numerology of 13.

This shortest day of the year in the northern hemisphere, completing the three-day period of the winter solstice when the rising Sun 'stands still' on the horizon, is the time of the rebirth of the solar/soular hero who offers new hope to the world.

In the Druidic lunar calendar, totalling 364 days and comprising 13 'moonths' of 28 days each, the sidereal lunar cycle as measured against the stars, this is the one day which they called 'out of time' and which reconciled the lunar and solar year.

It was on this day that we were to 'turn the 13th master key at Avebury'.

And as Ray had revealed in Hawaii, it was on this day that the Sun would become conjunct with the foot of Ophiuchus, the 13th zodiac sign, and thus the centre of the Galaxy. Momentously, as we'd discovered, such a conjunction does not happen every year. The wobble of the Earth about her axis meant that this was the first time in nearly 26,000 years that this conjunction was happening.

We finally knew why the guidance of the Elohim had specified this day and this place. And through our global quest with the Soular Discs we understood the significance of the transformational harmonic of 12 into 13. But the answer to one final question had continued to elude us. What was the 'master key' and how would we 'turn' it?

Geomancer Richard Leviton's insights again brought the answer. In the foreword to *The Galaxy on Earth*, he repeats the Hermetic dictum: 'The key is as above, so below and in the middle too.' That dictum came from the legendary teachings of the being known to the Romans as Hermes Trimegestes, Hermes the Thrice Greatest. The roots of this wisdom tradition date back to ancient Egypt and to Thoth, my lifelong spiritual guide.

As I read that simple phrase, it was the last few words – 'and in the middle too' – that gave me the answer. I laughed as I realized that Thoth had veiled my own insight of the reality that *we* are the master key.

*****

The energetic essence of the Harmonic Concordance offers an ever-present choice for us to individually embody ascended awareness. At a collective level, it continued to resonate through to the solar eclipse of 23 November, the completion of the 12th sidereal 'moonth' of the Druidic year and then on through the 13th 'moonth' to this 'day out of time'.

At 9.43 a.m. universal time on 23 December, the Sun and New Moon were conjunct in the sky and, through the archetypal healing essence of Asclepius/Ophiuchus, with the galactic centre.

At Avebury, our turning of the master key was to open the umbilical portal to the opportunity for a collective physical realization of Heaven on Mother Earth – the HoME-coming to the wholeness of who we really are through our human experience.

*****

Arriving early at Avebury on a cool quiet morning, I gave thanks to the spiritual guardian of this sacred place, who has taught me so much and continues to do so. I also marvelled as I finally and fully appreciated the significance and service of her guardianship over the millennia.

Welcoming our many friends and fellow travellers, we walked together to the Cove, the ancient grail of the Michael and Mary energies within the great henge, and formed a circle around and including its two remaining sarsen bastions. We each then offered our highest intentions for healing and wholeness.

Everyone present had arrived at this place and at this time after an inner and outer journey of many lifetimes. Each had undertaken to play a unique role on behalf of our wider collective. I invited each person to hear and listen to their own inner voice, and as they did so, everyone moved to their own special place within the microcosm of our Galaxy embodied by Avebury henge. It was as though each person was now becoming a star, connecting with the consciousness of the Galaxy through the cosmic umbilical cord of Avebury to complete the hologram of awakening and the physical embodiment of our HoME-coming.

As I felt my own connection deep within, I remembered an affirmation and prayer which had been created for the United Nations environmental programme. During many of our rainbow-bridge meditations around the world over the last eight years all of those present had spoken these words together:

We join with the Earth and each other
To bring new life to the land
To restore the waters
To refresh the air.

We join with the Earth and each other
To renew the forests
To care for the plants
To protect the creatures.

We join with the Earth and each other
To celebrate the seas
To rejoice in the sunlight
To sing the song of the stars.

We join with the Earth and each other
To recreate the human community
To promote justice and peace
To remember our children.

We join with the Earth and each other,
We join together as many and diverse expressions
Of One Loving Mystery, for the healing of the Earth
And the renewal of all Life.

As I felt the memory of these words resonate within me, our many voices came together to open the portal of the One heart.

*****

From the beginning of our Soular Disc journeys, the vision granted me by the Elohim was that our individual and group healing would ripple out and support our collective process – that the few of us able to physically connect to the Discs would be the representatives of the many.

After Australia, the remaining journeys, while offering ongoing choices for personal transformation, brought forward more and more opportunities for us to be the channels for collective and archetypal healing too.

We are ever more re-membering who we *really* are and that we co-create our realities. Thanks to our ability to communicate on a global level, we are able to form rainbow bridges of collective intent with our prayers and affirmations. We are each able to add our unique voice to the One heart and reconcile the Heaven of our spiritual nature with the Earth of our human journey.

But ultimately, it begins and ends with each of us and the choices we now make. Every one of us can choose to connect to the loving energies that are now available to us.

It may be the greatest challenge of our lives to take the leap of faith that is required to listen to and trust our inner voice. But it is that voice that speaks the wisdom of our heart. We can deny it and continue to live in the pain of past patterns – indeed, they can appear to be our comfort blanket in an uncertain world – or we can recognize that they are the cages of a self-imposed prison, whose door we can now open.

Each of us, when we are willing to hear and listen, knows in the depth of our being what we need to heal, and for many of us it may be a pattern, perhaps lifetimes old, of abandonment, abuse, betrayal, denial or rejection. Finding the compassion, clarity and courage to heal ourselves of these wounds is our gift to the collective healing of humanity.

Great spiritual masters have incarnated in the past as way-showers in embodying unconditional love and the experience of unity consciousness while in human form. We are ourselves now able to manifest this shift in awareness – or ascension – both personally and on an inclusive and collective level.

In the Christian tradition, this is the time of the prophesied 'second coming'. As the elders say, however, '*we* are the ones we've been waiting for' to embody our collective awakening into christed consciousness.

Each of us is a unique aspect of our collective journey home to the wholeness of who we really are, and our choices co-create our reality, at every moment, through our thoughts, feelings, words and actions, large and small.

*****

The path to our inner and outer freedom is one that has been trodden by all legendary and spiritual soular heroes. It is a path that each of us, travelling companions all, can now undertake.

And we have the support of all the realms of the Cosmos as we take our faltering steps towards our cosmic destiny.

The global journey in search of our collective destiny – not only that of humanity, but also of Gaia and our entire Soular System – reveal the age-old understanding of this path:

- Accept responsibility for our choices
- Choose love rather than fear
- In-to-great light and shadow and see beyond their polarities
- Consciously align with the flow of the Cosmos
- Live in the now
- Respect the conscious Cosmos and all its realms
- Intuitively listen to our higher selves

- Express loving truth
- Discern rather than judge
- Honour all experience without condemning, condoning or colluding
- Enact the golden rule in thought, speech and action
- Embody the em-powerment of cosmic service.

With nine years to the day until the December solstice of 2012, the time the ancient Maya and many mystics deem to be the birth-date of a collective shift of consciousness, the galactic portal is open and the cosmic blueprint of galactic and unity awareness is activated to support our way forward and the choice to embody our destiny.

ALONE TO ALL-ONE

This true story of our global odyssey has no end.

Since 23 December 2003, those who undertook its mission continue the path that we are all travelling together – as do we all. For each of us our journey is unique and yet we are all moving towards the unity of a common destination – a homecoming to the wholeness of who we really are.

As for myself, in the days following the opening of the galactic portal, I felt bereft. It seemed that my guidance had deserted me and I was left unsure of the way ahead. In my aloneness, I began to realize an energetic shift was taking place within me. Gradually, I understood that what I had perceived as being outside myself was becoming embodied within. And as the days became weeks, it was as though I was energetically pregnant with a new way of being.

By the autumn equinox, nine months after the opening of the galactic portal, I birthed within myself a knowing deeper than ever before that we are ultimately All-One – an awareness that required a fundamental transformation of how I perceived myself and my relationship with the Cosmos.

But as the following weeks and months unfolded, I experienced a roller-coaster of emotions, at one moment feeling empowered and fearless and the next profoundly vulnerable.

Gradually, as I integrated this new level of awareness, I established a balance within myself, and the energetic connection with the universal heart of my 8th chakra and the higher transpersonal chakras continued to strengthen and expand.

My work moved on to its next level. Invitations to share my understanding of the universal heart and our unity energy field began to arrive. Such an offer from the College of Psychic Studies led to my offering universal heart-centred soul healing sessions there and progressively around the world.

With my PhD thesis completed, invitations to write books also now came. The Elohim had guided me to write the true story of our 12 journeys and I completed the first draft in early summer 2004. Later in the year Hay House approached me and I offered them the manuscript of the book.

Everything felt right, but while they were enthusiastic about my work, to my surprise and disappointment they declined to publish the book.

Within days of that setback, another publisher, O Books, approached me to write a different book that reconciled science and spirit, and the following year *The Wave* was published.

In the meantime Hay House contacted me again and this time commissioned my second book, *The 8th Chakra*, which was published at the June solstice of 2006.

I had thought that the 12 journeys were complete, but to my shock, in the spring of 2006 the Elohim called me to a 13th pilgrimage. As if to validate the call and with perfect timing, within weeks Hay House confirmed that they now wished to go ahead with the book of the journeys – to include the 13th, whose path we were yet to tread…

CHAPTER 13

The 13th Journey

CHAPTER 13

THE 13th JOURNEY:
TURKEY, EGYPT AND ISRAEL

March and October 2006

Even in March, the heat of the early afternoon Sun made staying in the shade a definitely preferable option.

Following my higher guidance, Tony and I had travelled to this remote part of what is now south-eastern Turkey in search of the seed-point of an ancient schism in our collective psyche. Standing amidst the still impressive ruins of Harran, a vital centre and nexus for ideas and trade four millennia ago, we had come to connect energetically with the beginnings of the story of Abraham, the patriarch of the three world religions of Judaism, Christianity and Islam.

This now arid region from which spring the headwaters of the rivers Tigris and Euphrates is also being perceived by archaeologists as the likely setting of the biblical Garden of Eden. And recently-discovered ritual centres dating back an estimated 11,500 years – two-and-a-half times the age of the pyramids of Egypt – testify to its ancient significance and sanctity.

It was at Ur, which some scholars now believe refers to the nearby town of Urfa, rather than the far distant Ur of Mesopotamia, that Abraham first heard the word of the consciousness described most often in the Bible as 'the Lord'. And it was from Harran that he and his tribal family set out on the journey that many generations later would culminate in his descendants settling in the land promised by that guidance.

We were here on a quest to understand the nature of the spiritual direction received by Abraham and the identity of the being that came to be known to the Hebrew people as YHWH, Jehovah, and to the followers of Islam as Allah.

It is the essence of the guidance of YHWH that, as narrated in the Bible to Abraham and the bloodline of the patriarchs that followed him, continued to Moses and on to David, Solomon and the biblical prophets. In a very tangible form, it is embodied in the Jewish people and their perceived covenant with the land once known as Canaan and now as Israel.

In the service to healing the seemingly intransigent rift between the three faiths descended from Abraham and sowing the seeds of a yearned-for peace, we were here to ask the fundamental questions, 'Who is YHWH? And what does He want?'

*****

The biblical Book of Genesis relates that Abraham and his wife Sarah were unable to have children. Reaching the end of a long life, but still eager to continue his family bloodline, Abraham was encouraged by Sarah to father a child by her Egyptian maidservant Hagar.

The Bible relates how the then pregnant Hagar despised Sarah for being unable to conceive and how Sarah, with Abraham's approval, dealt 'hardly with her'. Exiled in the wilderness, Hagar saw an angel, who told her to return to her mistress Sarah. She did, and subsequently gave birth to a son, Ishmael – who was to be recognized as the patriarch of the Arabic peoples, the founding followers of Islam.

Thirteen years later, the Lord again appeared to Abraham and in covenanting to him and his descendants the land of Canaan, declaimed He would 'be a God to thee and to thy seed after thee'.

In doing so, the Lord also stated that Sarah and Abraham would have a child, despite Sarah being many years beyond childbearing age. The Bible narrates that while Abraham and Sarah literally fell about laughing at this prophecy, Sarah did miraculously conceive and bore a son, Isaac.

It was to the bloodline of Isaac, and Isaac alone, that the Lord then covenanted the land of Canaan. And while the Bible relates that Abraham and Hagar's son Ishmael was blessed with fruit-fulness, it is to this ancient choice that the schism between Judaism and Islam can be traced.

*****

Before journeying to Turkey, I'd received an e-mail from a woman named Sarah, who, echoing the events of four millennia ago, also had a young son named Isaac. Informing me that Isaac had been diagnosed with a rare and serious blood disorder, she asked for any insights I might have and for my prayers for her son.

When I explained to her what was unfolding about the blood-line of Abraham and the schism, she too had a deep sense that the healing of her own son would be connected with that archetypal healing.

I suddenly realized that the healing also required the reconcil-iation of the two mothers, Sarah and Hagar. And I understood how the schism had involved a rift in the expression of the divine feminine.

Months later, with young Isaac undergoing his medical treat-ment, I was still pondering the explicit question 'What does YHWH want?' and its implicit plea to enable reconciliation and peace to manifest.

As I struggled to find an answer, I woke from a dreamless night with the word 'Shekinah' reverberating in my mind.

A dim memory of the name stirred deep within me, but it was only by logging onto an Internet search that insight surged through me, as though an inner light had been switched on.

*****

To understand the nature and significance of the Shekinah, I first needed to attune further to YHWH himself and to trace the continuation of His covenant with the bloodline of Isaac.

Biblical scholars place the time of Abraham and Isaac as around 4,000 years ago. The deity appearing to Abraham and referred to by the Bible as 'the Lord', 'El' or 'El Shaddei' is now generally considered to be synonymous with the high god of the Canaanites. Indeed, the Bible refers to the Lord in ways that strongly suggest the perception of His being *a* god amongst gods – but more powerful and able to prevail over the other deities.

Seven centuries later, amidst their tribulations in Egypt, the Lord of the Hebrews reconfirmed the covenant, this time with Moses and his people and in a much more powerful and indeed warlike way than before. And when asked His name, for the first time the reply came: 'YHWH – I Am Who I Am.'

While the god of Abraham appeared willing to discuss and even negotiate the outcome of worldly events, the god of Moses was not to be gainsaid. Enforcing His authority through fear, He now even described himself as 'a jealous god' requiring the Israelites to worship Him – 'and no other god'.

Despite their apparent differences, Moses was able to convince his people that YHWH was the god of the patriarchs. The prowess of YHWH, mediated through the tenacious leadership of Moses, enabled the flight of the Exodus from Egypt and ultimately, after the long years of wandering in the wilderness, brought the Israelites to the 'promised land' of Canaan. And in harnessing the destructive strength of YHWH through the technology of the Ark of the Covenant, they overcame the indigenous Canaanites and established the beginnings of Israel.

By early in the first millennium BCE Israel had become a united nation under the kingship of David. With Jerusalem established as its capital, David's son Solomon consecrated the first temple dedicated to YHWH. It was here that the presence of the Shekinah was invited to reside.

While Judaic scholars continue to debate the meaning of the word *Shekinah*, usually translated as 'the presence of God', the word is innately female and is essentially the divine feminine principle manifest in the world.

I could now perceive her presence in the story of the Israelites, who continued, however, to have a problematic relationship with YHWH. And three centuries after the founding of the temple, amidst increasing corruption, growing political turmoil and the worship of other deities within the precincts of the temple itself, the consciousness of the Shekinah was deemed to have departed from Jerusalem.

Within two generations Assyrian invasions had scattered 10 of the 12 tribes of the Israelite people, losing them to history, had driven the remaining Israelites into exile and had destroyed the temple.

With the Israelites' eventual return some 50 years later, a second temple was built on the ruins of the first and the Shekinah implored to return to its inner sanctum, the holy of holies. It was this second temple, magnificently reconstructed by King Herod the Great, that stood at the time of Jesus.

The original teachings of Jesus, now progressively emerging with the discoveries and translations of books excised from the New Testament canon, show the inclusion of the divine feminine as an integral aspect of the cosmic trinity through which consciousness and all phenomena are manifest.

The Shekinah, in the essence of the Holy Ghost, is embodied at the heart of these teachings. And the reconciliation and balance of masculine, feminine and child principles on individual, collective and cosmic levels is ultimately the portal to christed or unity awareness – the revelation of the One through which the diversity of the Cosmos is expressed.

The turmoil of continuing Jewish clashes with Rome led to the uprising of 66 CE. And mystical tradition describes the Shekinah as again leaving the temple at this time and abiding energetically on the Mount of Olives, to the east of Jerusalem, for three years before ascending at what is now known as the Shrine of the Ascension.

Four years after her departure from the holy of holies, the Romans finally captured Jerusalem. Utterly demolishing the temple, following further revolts they imposed increasing subjugation before finally dispersing the Jewish people – a diaspora that lasted almost two millennia until the re-establishment of the state of Israel in 1948.

*****

As I continued to attune to the biblical YHWH I realized that the primordial nature of His consciousness was territorial – profoundly rooted in the land covenanted to the Israelites. The divine feminine embodied by the Shekinah was, however, universal.

The diaspora enabled and indeed mandated that to retain their sense of identity and their hoped-for reconciliation with the land of Israel, each Jewish person had to continue to engage with the Shekinah. Specifically, at each Shabbat she is invited into the inner heart of every Jewish family, wherever they may be. Thus, for two millennia, in the Shekinah, the presence of the divine feminine as inherent and immanent in all manifestation has been progressively embraced in a way that far transcends the territorial nature of the biblical YHWH.

In 1948, history repeated itself as the modern state of Israel was born. As in the ancient overthrow of the Canaanites, the Palestinian people were displaced as the territorial essence of the covenant between YHWH and the Jewish people was re-energized. But in the perceived absence of the Jerusalem temple, the knowledge of whose very position on the city's Temple Mount had been lost, it seems that the Shekinah was not invited to return and the divine feminine remained exiled.

*****

At last I began to perceive an answer to the question, 'What does YHWH want?'

As I sensed the presence of the Elohim and Shekinah guiding me on a continuing inner journey of discovery, I now felt the yearning not only of the territorial entity but of the higher transcendent essence of YHWH. With the ancient covenant once more reborn in conflict, I now understood that YHWH sought release from this pattern of the past, a re-soulution made possible by the return of the Shekinah, and, with her reconciling grace, to establish not the ancient temple with its blood sacrifices and patriarchal authority, but a metaphysical temple denoting the birth of a new and transcendent Jerusalem.

I sensed that the Shekinah's return would open a portal of possibility – the manifestation of a holy city, not of one faith or faction, but the heritage, hope and re-soulution of all humanity.

As the vision before me enlarged, I gained a numinous perception of Allah, rather than the being compared in the Koran to the god of Abraham. And I also became aware of how the perception of the God of the Christian faith was maturing from a patriarchal and often-feared deity to a God of love, as taught by Jesus himself.

The mystical followers of all three faiths are seeking to transcend the personal conception of supreme reality and in so doing, at their most profound, embrace the transcendence of God and thus abjure the illusory divisions and dogmatic limitations of their religions.

The followers of all three traditions stand at a crossroads. Do they embrace God as the prime mover of an interrelated conscious Cosmos, ultimately cosmic mind wherein we are both creation and co-creators? Or will they choose to hold on to ancient perceptions that glimpsed the divine through the inevitable lenses of the cultures of two millennia ago?

*****

The stories of the journeying of the biblical patriarchs and prophets up to the time of the Exodus is interwoven with the history of Egypt. At the birth of Jesus, the Bible describes how Mary and Joseph, escaping the tyranny of King Herod, found sanctuary there. And now this ancient land is a secular Islamic state.

All three faiths have their ideational genesis here too, for ancient Egypt birthed the idea of monotheism through the then perceived heresy of the pharaoh Akhenaten.

I hoped that the ancient wisdom residing in this sacred land would proffer deeper insights and guidance, as it had so profoundly before. And so we, like so many pilgrims before us, made ready to journey to Egypt.

*****

In a wholly interrelated conscious Cosmos, all that we term 'reality' is integral. And manifestation arises from intention at multiple levels of the cosmic hologram. Thus, as energy medicine acknowledges, healing begins and energetically flows from its point of supra-physical causality.

To heal the archetypal schisms that separate us, we too need to acknowledge their underlying causation and, as co-creators of our realities, instigate our intention for the healing to occur.

We can only take responsibility for our choices at the level of awareness we have when we make those choices. But, as we had directly experienced during the journeys, there are now energetic levels of awareness newly available to us that can expand our perception and enable us to see beyond the limitations of our ego-based fears to dream into manifestation a new way of being.

As we had discovered, the portal to this higher awareness and the re-membering of who we really are is the 8th chakra of the universal heart. Opening our minds, hearts and will to the reconciliation of the divine masculine, feminine and child consciousness within us enables us to heal at the most profound levels of our personal and collective soul.

*****

While initially my intention had only been to return to Egypt, I now knew that the journey needed to culminate where the schism continued to play itself out at its most seemingly intractable level – the ancient land of Canaan that we now know as Israel.

As if what was already unfolding was not enough, a further understanding began to emerge of how the schism was manifesting a deeper rift in our human psyche that could be traced back to the beginnings of our human story and the bloodline of our entire human family.

A seemingly separate but in reality a deeply interwoven thread of this need to delve further arose in a call I received some weeks before leaving for Turkey. The call opened up the psychic healing of a bloodline that spanned nearly eight centuries, involving Thomas de Cantilupe, a 13th-century saint, his friend Richard Plantagenet, Earl of Cornwall, and Richard's two sons, Henry and Edmund.

Thomas, it turned out, was a leader of the mysterious order of Knights Templar. And the spiritual presence of all four knights was to provide vigilant protection throughout the forthcoming journey and reveal secret knowledge of our human heritage. For we now discovered that the esoteric knowledge of the Templars also related to the involvement of the extraterrestrial Annunaki in the hidden history of humanity – something we'd explored and experienced in China five years before.

Only days after receiving these psychic insights from St Thomas, Tony and I were in the area of modern Turkey that is being progressively viewed as the site of the biblical Garden of Eden. Here the reptilian consciousness of the Annunaki being known as Enki, the serpent in the garden who encouraged Eve to eat of the Tree of Knowledge, stirred powerful memories within me. Attuning to both emergent streams of awareness, that of YHWH and the Annunaki, I could now sense how the former had offered a cultural conduit for the intentions of the latter.

In China, we had attuned to how the Annunaki leaders, the brothers Enki and Enlil, had intended two radically different destinies for the genetically modified hominid-Annunaki race of humanity. At the culmination of that journey, as we had activated the Soular Disc at Rawak, the two had been reconciled at the highest energetic level, thus opening the portal for their reconciliation to eventually manifest in the physical world.

And now our journey to Turkey in service to the healing of these fundamental rifts came at a time when the desert of this ancient Eden was beginning to bloom. A huge project aimed at diverting the waters of the rivers of Eden was creating a vast matrix of irrigation canals and channels – the Garden was becoming fertile once again.

*****

When we had decided to return to Egypt, as before we had planned to journey the full length of the country, from the temples of Abu Simbel in the south to the pyramids and Sphinx of Giza in the north.

While that first pilgrimage had only taken place five-and-a-half years earlier, it felt a lifetime ago, so much on both my inner and outer levels having been transformed in the interim.

The 13th note of the ancient chromatic musical scale completes one octave and begins the next. I now sensed that this extended journey, the 13th of our global quest to discover and heal our hidden heritage and reveal our cosmic destiny, was to complete the mission Tony and I had begun all those millennia ago in Lemuria. Yet I was beginning to have a foreboding of what the Elohim might ask of me. As to whether it would also represent the first 'note' of a higher octave of awareness, I had neither hope nor expectation. I only knew I needed to show up!

To add to my sense of disquiet, for weeks my shoulders and neck had become ever more painful. Nothing could alleviate it. It was almost as though my head was being torn from my body – or perhaps being reattached?

*****

When Justina, our fellow traveller from the first Soular Disc journey to Egypt in 2001, had originally offered to organize our return, we'd agreed that early- to mid-October would be a good time, given the seasonal heat. We decided on a 13-day trip and, given the limitations of the flight schedules, agreed on the dates of 2–14 October.

As had become usual, it was only in hindsight that the significance of the dates and their incredible synchronicities unfolded. Journeying from the USA, Australia, Austria and the UK, the first members of our group of 27 fellow travellers arrived in Cairo on 2 October, the Jewish Day of Atonement. This holiest of Jewish days commemorates the atonement of the Jews' turning away from YHWH at Mount Sinai and the subsequent rededication to their covenant.

It was the perfect date for us to commence our journey.

*****

The following day, 3 October, was equally synchronous, given the guiding presence of St Thomas de Cantilupe in our unfolding story. For of all days, this was his feast day!

As everyone had already undertaken tiring flights to be here, we'd decided that this first full day would be spent getting to know each other and anchoring the intention of our journey by visiting three sites sacred in turn to Judaism, Christianity and Islam.

The energies of this trinity of holy places – the synagogue of Elijah, the hanging church (so called due to its construction atop a prior building) and the Mohammed Ali mosque – gifted us further insights into how the archetypal consciousness of the cosmic masculine, feminine and child principles continue to play out on individual and collective levels.

We also appreciated the significance of our group being 27 in number – 3 x 3 x 3 – a trinity of trinities. This was powerfully resonant with how we would continue to experience the reconciliation and healing of these energetic aspects ourselves. Throughout the 13 journeys of our odyssey, the trinity expressed through our hearts, minds and will continued to energetically open the universal heart of the 8th chakra, the portal to our personal and collective re-membering.

Now, in attuning to the traditions of these three faiths, we perceived how each of them emphasized one of these energetic principles on a generic level. And we could see the global empowerment that could be energized by their creative co-operation if their followers are able to reconcile the schisms of culture and prejudice that has separated them for so long.

In describing the relationship of the Old Testament patriarchs with YHWH, the Bible stresses the ways in which they sought to negotiate with him. Throughout that narration and the millennia since, it has been the understanding of the Word and Law of God that Judaism has emphasized – the way of the mind. The teachings of Jesus as embodied by the Christian faith, however, focus on the power of love and compassion – the way of the heart. Whereas Islam, in the special significance it gives to equality and justice, stresses the submission of human purpose to the higher purpose of Allah – the way of the will.

Each of the cosmic principles of this fundamental trinity is also expressed through the consciousness of the divine masculine, feminine and child, whose energetic balance is also a requisite for reconciliation on personal and collective levels. In this way, the ongoing mainstream traditions of all three faiths are as yet out of balance. Continuing to exert religious authority through men, they exclude women to a lesser or greater degree from participation and decision making, even to the point of segregating the act of worship itself.

Now, as we directly experienced this physical and energetic separation for ourselves and felt its resonance throughout our collective psyche, we all appreciated how such segregation has constrained the expression of the Shekinah in every one of us, regardless of whether we were born male or female.

And so is it any wonder that exponentially increasing numbers of Western women free to follow their own spiritual path are doing so, liberated from the constraints of organized faiths that continue to treat them as second-class citizens?

*****

After a further day of exploration, we journeyed on to the far south of Egypt. Here, as on previous journeys, we began to connect energetically with the principles of consciousness the ancient Egyptians called *neterw*.

These archetypal beings, the so-called gods and goddesses of Egypt, were to be our guides as personally and as a group we underwent our own inner journeys of discovery and healing.

*****

After a day visiting the powerful temples of Rameses II and his wife Nefertari at Abu Simbel, I settled down to sleep on the night of 5 October with no intimation of what was to become a dark night of the soul.

Awakening suddenly from an overwhelmingly distressing dream, I found every aspect of it etched on my mind and heart and I began to weep silent tears.

In the dream, as though the reality of it was imminent, Tony and I were our familiar selves and then, with no warning, I died. I was unclear as to the cause.

The scene then shifted. It seemed to be only a short while later, but I saw Tony with someone else. Present but unnoticed, as I looked around I could sense that I was forgotten – there was no sign that I had ever existed. Tony and the woman he was with clearly adored each other. I could vividly see her face and, shocked, realized she was one of our fellow travellers on this journey.

I lay in the dark next to my sleeping husband, but now, it seemed, separated from him by a vast abyss of pain.

Over the coming hours, I realized I had no choice but to go into the heart of the darkness to seek the understanding it was offering me.

At first light, I fell into an uneasy sleep for a couple of hours until it was time to get up and face the day.

*****

That morning we were to visit the temple of Isis. As was the case for the temples of Abu Simbel, this had also been transported stone by stone from its original position to save it from the rising waters caused by the creation of the Aswan High Dam some years before. Set on a beautiful island, it consecrated two aspects of the divine feminine represented by the *neter* Isis and her fellow goddess Hathor.

As the two of us sat together, I shared with Tony some but not all of my experience of the previous night. Still raw with emotion, I couldn't yet bring myself to tell him the identity of the woman I'd seen him with in my dream.

Continuing to be open to a deeper awareness, that evening we'd planned to return to the temple for its spectacular sound and light show. The first stage of the show invited the audience to follow the narration inside the temple precincts. But as it ended and we were being directed by the temple guards to move outside for the second part of the show, I suddenly felt an overpowering urge to continue into the inner sanctum dedicated to Isis.

Despite the guards' insistence, four of us, including Tony and me, were able to persuade them, helped of course by a payment of baksheesh, to allow us to spend some precious time at the altar dedicated to her.

Afterwards, trembling with the energies of Isis, I walked outside to hear the narrator begin to tell the audience of the relationship between Isis, Hathor and the *neter* Horus. He began to relate an ancient myth whose significance I had not understood until now. He spoke of how Isis had given birth to Horus, but explained that it was Hathor who then raised the cosmic child and later became his consort.

The two goddesses, each an aspect of the divine feminine, were sundered by their mutual jealousy over their relationships with Horus – an aspect of the story I'd never heard before, but which now resonated deeply within me.

Still reverberating with the presence of Isis, I could suddenly feel her and my own jealousy as the pain of the dream of the night before returned.

*****

At breakfast the following morning, Deborah, our fellow traveller and the woman in my dream, asked if we could have a quiet word together.

She told me that I had appeared in her dreams, and as we discussed our experiences it became clear to us both that she and I were respectively embodying the essence of Hathor and Isis.

We continued to share how we each had played out these patterns of mother and lover on conditional and dysfunctional levels in our own patterns of behaviour. And, weeping, we both realized that we now had the opportunity to heal a deep sundering in our own psyches and to be in service to such healing on its archetypal level. In energetically reconciling the Hathor and Isis within ourselves, we could enable the divine feminine to birth the cosmic child embodied in this ancient tradition by the archetypal Horus.

And with a cathartic release, I could now see that my dream presaged not my physical death but a dying to the old way of expressing the divine feminine and a reconciliation of Isis and Hathor within myself.

*****

In the Jewish calendar of 2006, 7 October was the first Day of Tabernacles, the day commemorating the enthronement of YHWH. To the ancient Egyptians, the pharaoh was both king and god and deemed to be the embodiment of Horus. So how perfect, once again, that on this day we were to visit the great temple at Edfu dedicated to Horus – and were now able to initiate and celebrate the birth of this cosmic child within ourselves.

Approaching the temple, I asked where the quietest place would be for us as a group to undertake a ceremony. Sabry, our wonderful guide, without knowing our purpose, said without hesitation, 'The *mamessi*.' This chapel to the south of the temple was dedicated to the emergence of the divine – in essence, it was the birthplace of the cosmic child.

We came together standing in a silent circle, with Deborah and me calling upon Tony to stand alongside us to represent the trinity of Hathor, Isis and Horus. We then invoked the reconciliation of the divine feminine and the birthing of the cosmic child within each person in turn. As each man and woman inwardly acknowledged this intention for themselves, I could feel the beating wings of Horus surge into flight as the co-creative essence of the cosmic child was embodied.

*****

The next day we set out to explore Luxor, the religious centre known as Thebes to the ancient Egyptians.

In the already stultifying heat of the late morning and early afternoon we emerged from the pharaonic tombs of the Valley of the Kings and made our way to the mortuary temple of Hatshepsut. While the male pharaohs of Egypt gained their legitimacy through marriage, very few women, of whom Hatshepsut is perhaps the best known, were pharaohs in their own right.

We walked slowly towards the temple and the statue of hawk-headed Horus at its threshold. As I gazed ahead, I recalled the time when I had been here only days after the infamous massacre of tourists by Islamic fundamentalists in 1997. Then we had sought to release the spirits of those who had died and to heal the energies of this sacred place.

Now, as we walked towards a small chapel of the *neter* Anubis within the temple, I remembered that many of those who perished had forlornly sought refuge here. Yet the ancient role of Anubis as the guide of departed souls and the way-shower to their resurrection rendered his presence proper.

Standing in the shadows of the chapel, together we attuned to the energies of the temple and opened ourselves to higher guidance. As we then shared our impressions, we became aware that something was being asked of us. While many spiritually focused groups had visited this place since 1997, we had the strong sense that the temple now needed to be reconsecrated as it had been when first constructed over three millennia ago.

As we had experienced again and again, once the causes of an energetic imbalance are acknowledged and understood and the intention to heal made, the healing itself is often of the utmost simplicity, with no need for dramatic or complex ritual. To honour the spiritual request asked of us, all we needed to do was to offer lotus essence at the temple threshold, as we sensed the ancient priests would have, together with our heartfelt intentions that the sanctity of this place be restored.

As a final act of service, however, I felt the need to walk up the great ramp to the uppermost level of the temple.

Hatshepsut and her son-in-law and successor the pharaoh Thothmoses III are reputed to have had a difficult relationship, with Thothmoses reportedly defacing many of the images of the queen after her death.

As I entered the courtyard, a temple guard insistently called me to one side. Encouraging me to step over the rope that was meant to hold visitors back, he took me to a niche cut into the bedrock of the cliff. Looking up, I saw the portrayal of Thothmoses III, here of all places, in the mortuary temple of his old enemy.

As I gazed at his image, I suddenly realized that I had been brought here to witness and to understand that he and Hatshepsut were now reconciled too.

*****

Returning to Abydos once more after nearly six years, I felt again the power of the Soular Disc resonating within me as we walked towards the magnificent façade of the temple of Osiris.

In the sudden transition from the bright sunlight to the dark shadow of the temple, I heard an inner call to go on to the inner sanctum housing the three chapels dedicated to the trinity of Osiris, Isis and Horus.

Each time I had been here before, I had experienced a personal epiphany. But today I realized that my purpose was solely to facilitate that for each of my fellow travellers. As always, each was free to explore wherever their own inner guidance called them. But for those who chose to do so, we attuned ourselves to each of the three *neterw* and then I led the way through the temple and along the ancient corridor that led to the Oseirion, the so-called tomb of Osiris and the epicentre of the Soular Disc energies.

Once again I found myself walking in the dazzling sunlight onto the ramp leading down to the monolithic Oseirion. This time, I couldn't believe my eyes. The water that now covered its floor was a colour unlike any I'd ever seen. On previous occasions, the subterranean floor had been covered with clear turquoise-tinged water. But now the water was a vibrant, almost luminescent, green, teeming with algae.

For millennia the myth of Osiris depicting his life, death and resurrection was played out each year in Egypt's seasonal round. The greening of the land following the Nile flood and its subsidence embodied the resurgent Osiris. And as I gazed, mesmerized, I could feel that regeneration within myself.

*****

Each evening of the journey we all came together to share our experiences and insights of the day, a co-creative exploration that brought us ever closer to each other. By now the theme of the resoulution of masculine, feminine and child energies was powerfully and joyfully familiar to us, richly embodied through both our personal experiences and those of our group.

A further insight was also continuing to express itself. We reminded ourselves that legend described the head of Osiris as being safeguarded at Abydos and that after his murder and dismemberment by Set, Isis brought his body parts here to be magically reassembled and finally reconnected to his head. Throughout the allegories of ancient myth, the head expressed mind and power and its symbolic removal a sundering of both.

Some of the group, including me, were experiencing severe neck pain, headaches and pressure at the base of our skulls, the location of the alter-major chakra. A few months earlier I'd received information suggesting that as part of the Annunaki agenda to control humanity the energies of this chakra had been shut down, thus curtailing our access to our higher mind. But now, as personally and collectively we are undertaking a profound process of re-membering, the alter-major chakra is reactivating and I intuitively knew that our physical pain would resolve itself when that realignment was complete.

And we realized that the resurgence of Osiris at Abydos, symbolizing that his head too was now reattached, was yet another way-shower to this archetypal healing of our psyche.

*****

Returning to Giza and standing on the highest point of the plateau, gazing across at the magnificent sight of the pyramids, I reflected on this 13th journey from its inception in Turkey eight months before and felt an enormous surge of love and gratitude for all those who had journeyed with us.

To a greater degree than ever before, I deeply sensed the presence of those discarnate beings who were also our fellow travellers and indeed our way-showers. And as I clairvoyantly looked around me, I saw the great community of spiritual pilgrims who had walked alongside us in service to re-soulution.

Patriarchs, pharaohs, prophets, saints and knights were now joined by another presence. Here of all places, a modern pharaoh of Egypt, its assassinated president Anwar Al Sadat, had once built a summerhouse. It was here that he first dreamed of the possibility of peace in the Middle East. Although the building has since been demolished, its foundations remain.

In seeking to manifest the peace of his dream, President Sadat negotiated and signed the Camp David Peace Agreement between Egypt and Israel in 1978 and, with his co-signatory Menachim Begin, became a recipient of the Nobel Peace Prize.

In sensing his presence I remembered that the Arabic word for peace, *salaam*, is poignantly similar to the Hebrew word, *shalom*.

Welcoming Sadat and inviting his companionship on our onward journey, Tony and I made our way back to the coach and on to the Great Pyramid. But before we did so, we gathered small pebbles together to form the word 'peace' in the sand beside the president's erstwhile home.

*****

Our initiation in the Great Pyramid was taking place on the 12th of the month, yet another reminder of how the unity awareness of our cosmic destiny embodied the energetic harmonic of 12 and the transformational 13.

We were again fortunate in having private access to this incredible place which, with its two companion pyramids, energetically embodied the cosmic trinity of male, female and child, and whose three inner chambers also offered a three-step initiatory process of integration.

The feeling of foreboding that had been ebbing and flowing since the beginning of this journey now strengthened, however, and I sensed that these next few hours would be pivotal to my own inner path. My fear of whether I would be able to energetically and physically undertake what the Elohim might ask of me both here and in Israel returned. And as I paused at the threshold, I knew this was the 13th step – the completion of an entire cycle of my own soular journey.

What I didn't know was how I would take that step and whether I would ever take another.

Each of us chose now our own path of initiation. Some immediately began to climb up the ascending passage to the so-called Queen's Chamber. Others continued upwards through the vaulted magnificence of the Grand Gallery to the King's Chamber. And others chose to begin their inner journey of discovery by traversing the descending passage into the strange and mysterious subterranean chamber.

Bowing low, I scampered down the 200-foot length of the descending passage to my own first-choice destination. Excavated from the bedrock beneath the pyramid, the inchoate form of the subterranean chamber embodies the infinite possibilities of the cosmic child in us all.

But as I clambered down the last step and stood here once again, I saw the entrance to the low passage that leads from the south-eastern corner of the chamber, tunnelling due south into the bedrock beneath the pyramid. Previously, a locked iron gate had always covered the entrance. But today, the gate was open and I could feel the blackness of the passageway calling me.

As I knelt down, ready to crawl along its length, I felt Tony's loving presence standing beside me. While he sensed no need to undertake this ordeal himself, he knew that I did and was prepared to stand vigil for me.

By the dim light of the small torch I carried with me, I made my slow way forward. Each heartbeat felt louder within me as I became oblivious to the outer world and returned to the void of the cosmic womb. Finally reaching the end of the long passage, I turned off the torch and curled up in a foetal position in the darkness.

In those moments, beyond the reach of time, my previous fear subsided as I was gently lulled into an all-pervasive peace of mind and heart that transcended the aloneness of my past and heralded the All-Oneness of my future.

*****

I returned to Tony and, climbing back up the descending passage, we went on together up to the Queen's Chamber.

As I sat quietly with my companions attuning to and embodying the gentle feminine energies here, I took this second step of integrating this new way of being.

Now ready to take the third and final step, Tony and I began our ascent of the magnificent Grand Gallery leading to the King's Chamber.

Realizing that time was moving on, as I stepped into this third chamber, I glanced at my watch to see that it was reading 12.00 midday – even this was exact!

Gradually, all our companions were making their way here. Some were sitting quietly attuning. Others had chosen to spend time in the so-called sarcophagus, the casket of solid granite within which, through the millennia, many initiates had gained profound insights.

Joining those standing around the sarcophagus, I energetically stood vigil while whoever wished to spent time within.

When no one else appeared to want to do so, I felt I could now take my own place there.

As I lay down and closed my eyes, I could hear voices toning around me, resonating ever more powerfully within the crystalline matrix of the perfectly proportioned granite-lined chamber and the sarcophagus itself. I felt my entire body reverberate as the waves of sound rose to an incredible crescendo more beautiful than I had ever experienced.

Suddenly, the roof of the chamber and the entire upper reaches of the pyramid disappeared and I could see in my inner vision not the brightness of the daylight outside but the velvet blackness of space awash with stars that sparkled like heavenly gems.

I felt my awareness become All-One with the Cosmos and a complete knowing of myself as a co-creator. And I heard the *neterw*, the star gods of the ancient Egyptians, welcoming me with the words, 'You now walk with us.'

*****

After a further day of integrating and sharing our experiences, we all recognized how profound our path had been on every level. And we knew that we were all now connected in a way that would call us at a soul level to journey on together.

And in embodying the unity awareness of All-Oneness within myself, I now was without fear of whatever might come.

With our companions leaving for home, Tony and I had arranged to stay on in Cairo for a further day before travelling on to Jerusalem on 15 October. With as yet no understanding of what we would be doing there, I had nevertheless been guided by the Elohim that we needed to culminate our healing work in Jerusalem overnight on 18 October and journey on to Megiddo the next morning to complete our pilgrimage.

Unbeknown to us when the timing for the journey had been agreed, our entire trip was to take place during the Islamic holy month of Ramadan. We then discovered that there is one night during Ramadan, the date of which changes every year, that is known as the Night of Destiny. It is said that during this night the gates of the heavens are opened and the angels hear and answer all prayers.

We were to discover that the guidance of the Elohim had already ensured that it was this night of all nights that we would culminate our healing work in Jerusalem. For the Night of Destiny this year would be 18 October.

*****

As Tony and I walked through the arrivals hall at Tel Aviv airport, the clock showed 13.00. And as we were about to catch a bus on to Jerusalem, the heavens opened in a rare and dramatic thunderstorm. Given that one of the names attributed to the biblical YHWH was El Shaddei, the god of thunder, we felt our arrival was being welcomed and we in turn welcomed the downpour.

In the Old City of Jerusalem, where we'd arranged to stay at the Knights' Palace Hotel, with its reputed connections back to Crusader times, we were soon joined by Rebecca and Anne, both of whom had felt a deep call to be here to undertake this work with us and share what was to come – whatever that might be!

*****

Our first priority was to explore the Old City and attune to the sites that was sacred to all three faiths. We trusted that this would allow us to follow the guidance of the Elohim and to understand how to invoke the return of the Shekinah and her transcendent reconciliation with YHWH.

Esoteric tradition gave us a clue. For it is said that when her essence departed Jerusalem in 66 BCE, the Shekinah left the temple's holy of holies and passed through the east gate of the city to the Mount of Olives. Three years later, she is said to have ascended from the Mount at what is now know as the Shrine of the Ascension – the same place from which Jesus is deemed to have ascended.

Such metaphysical traditions have also prophesied that both christed consciousness and the Shekinah will return to the temple's holy of holies the same way, along the path known as 'the messiah line'.

Given that the knowledge of where the temple was located on Temple Mount was lost to the Jewish people following their diaspora nearly two millennia ago, the location of its inner sanctum remains unknown. There are, however, historical texts and archaeological considerations from which three main theories have been derived as to its location, one of which we felt immediately drawn to.

Tradition points to the Shekinah's hoped-for return as retracing her departure, being a straight line from the Shrine of Ascension through the east gate of the Old City and on to the temple's holy of holies. When extended westwards within the Temple Mount, the pathway marked by the shrine and the gate passes directly through a small cupola raised over an outcrop of rock – the Dome of the Spirits. It is this place, to the north of the famous Dome of the Rock, that the so-called northern theory for the temple's location places its ancient holy of holies. And extending this line westwards leads to the most sacred monument in Christendom, the Church of the Holy Sepulchre.

In the time of Jesus, this site was a small rocky rise just outside the city walls. In the early 4th century, the hillside was excavated and the church built to house three of the most sacred locations of Christ's ministry – his crucifixion, burial and resurrection.

Continuing the line still further to the edge of the Old City, we were amazed to discover that it led directly to where we had arranged to stay – the Knights' Palace Hotel, with its historical connections to the secret order of our discarnate companions and guardians, the Templar knights St Thomas de Cantilupe and Richard, Edmund and Henry Plantagenet.

*****

I sensed the guidance of the Elohim becoming ever clearer now that we were actually present in Jerusalem. And, as Tony, Anne, Rebecca and I attuned together, we now understood that we had been called here to energetically reactivate the so-called messiah line and to invoke on the forthcoming Night of Destiny the return of the Shekinah.

Every step of this unfolding journey was now in service to the reconciliation and re-soulution of the divine feminine presence with YHWH in the holy of holies and the birthing of a transcendent hope for peace.

The next morning we set out for the Temple Mount,

When the Moslems conquered Jerusalem in the 7th century, they constructed the al-Aqsa mosque and the golden-domed Dome of the Rock here to commemorate the site as Mohammed's dream of his ascent to heaven. While the Mount is in Moslem East Jerusalem, it is under Jewish control, and with the ever-present tensions, heightened during the holy month of Ramadan, we didn't know whether we would be allowed even to visit the Mount, let alone have access to the two sites that were our intended destination. However, despite the tight security, we discovered that we could visit the Mount until the time for morning prayers, when we would have to leave.

Realizing our time was short, we focused on the two sites central to our quest – the east gate of the Old City and the Dome of the Spirits. In attuning to both, we intended to begin the geomantic process of preparing the messiah line for the return of the Shekinah.

At the eastern entrance to the Old City, Moslems had constructed the so-called Golden Gate in the 7th century over the earlier gate that had stood there at the time of Jesus and through which He had entered Jerusalem in triumph. In an attempt to prevent His prophesied second coming, this point of entrance, so significant to Christians, had been bricked up less than a century after its construction.

The gate has two arches and tradition tells that both the christed consciousness and the Shekinah will return through the more northern of the two.

We now appreciated that to fully embody our conscious intent we needed to be physically close to the Golden Gate. But whether that would be at all possible we had no idea.

Heading away from the crowds, we hurried down the flight of steps that led to the outer courtyard of the Mount and to the inner side of the gate, only to realize with disappointment that access to it at ground level was blocked off.

Wondering where to go now, we suddenly saw a flight of stairs winding up the northern side of the gate. And more significantly still, we saw a door at the top of the stairs leading onto the city wall directly above the gate – and the door was open!

Hardly believing what was happening, with no one else around, we clambered up the stairs and through the door. Now, within feet of the gate, I felt an overpowering urge to take a final step up onto the wall itself.

As I did, ahead of me, across the valley, rose the Mount of Olives and the Shrine of the Ascension. I realized that I was standing directly over the northern arch of the gate and that now was the moment to activate the energies of the messiah line from there to this point.

Seconds later, a guard who, unnoticed by us, had been sleeping in his cabin only a few feet from where we were, woke. It was now his turn to be hardly able to believe that anyone would be here!

As I inwardly felt the line activate, I knew it was time to leave. As we did, a large group of visitors saw us descending the stairs and headed quickly towards them, only to have the guard firmly close the door to prevent them from entering.

With little time left before we would be required to leave the Temple Mount, we made our way to the modest stone canopy known as the Dome of the Spirits, deemed to be the location of the inner sanctum, the holy of holies of the ancient temple. And here too we attuned to energize the line in preparation for the return of the Shekinah.

Our work here was done.

*****

Leaving Temple Mount, we made our way along the poignant length of the Via Dolorosa. This 'Way of Tears' is the path traditionally taken by Jesus from where He was tried to his crucifixion and burial. Along its length are the 14 stations of the cross, each marking a particular event in the suffering of His passion. At each station, we prayed for the release of all the religious schisms that had divided our human family for so long.

Finally we arrived at the Church of the Holy Sepulchre, which houses the last five stations. Another wonderful synchronicity had occurred before our journey when a dear friend, Sahar, had offered to introduce us to some of her family living in Jerusalem. How perfect that this Moslem family, renowned for their integrity, had been the gatekeepers of this ancient church for many generations!

Here, too, our heads bowed in supplication, we prayed for re-soulution and peace at each of the inner chapels dedicated to the final events of Jesus's life and burial.

But the place of His burial was also the place of His resurrection.

And here, as I stood on the energetic line of the messiah, as in the King's Chamber of the Great Pyramid, I embodied the unity awareness that He taught is our innate nature and the re-member-ing of which is our cosmic destiny.

A few yards away stands a simple stone basin that ancient mapmakers believed marks the centre of the world. While it was roped off to visitors at the time, our introduction to the gatekeeper permitted our entry and we stood around this ancient marker initi-ating our heartfelt intention that the re-soulution yet to come would radiate from here to all corners of the Earth.

As I inwardly asked for an outer sign to validate our inner work, I looked down and there on the marble floor lay a feather – the ancient symbol of ascension.

And as we made to leave, the inspiring tones of the liturgical song of praise 'Christ is Risen' arose from a choir of Russian pilgrims standing around the 13th station of the cross.

*****

The following day we made our way to the Mount of Olives and the Shrine of the Ascension.

As we walked through the open gate to the inner courtyard surrounding the shrine, again there were no other visitors. And with the guard otherwise occupied, we had the peace and time to energetically ready the way for the Shekinah to return.

As we were preparing to leave, it was no surprise that a large group of visitors arrived, and as we made our way out, they too began to sing a prayer of rejoicing.

*****

The day that would culminate in the Night of Destiny had arrived and I awoke with a profound sense of purpose and hope.

We had now realized that during the entire night there would be literally hundreds of thousands of Moslem worshippers on Temple Mount and that our own overnight vigil would take place on the rooftop of the Knights' Palace hotel. From there we would then go to the Mount of Olives to physically walk the messiah line from the Shrine of the Ascension to the Golden Gate to welcome the return of the Shekinah there at dawn.

Seven years earlier Tony had experienced a powerful psychic message when he was given the words:

Restore the temple,
Elucidate the knowledge,
Establish the love.

At the time, he had no understanding of its import. But now, its meaning felt prophetic and its reality imminent.

The four us joined hands on the rooftop overlooking the Old City of Jerusalem as we began our midnight vigil. I felt the presence of the many beings who had walked this journey of aeons with us to this moment when the schisms that had separated our human family for so long were ready to be healed at the level of their causation.

As I gazed to the east with my inner vision, I could see the discarnate community of peacemakers who had been our companions from the inception of this 13th journey. Almost like a bridal party accompanying the groom while he waits for his bride, I could sense their presence with that of YHWH at the holy of holies on Temple Mount. And I felt the deep bond of the loving presence of all our fellow travellers in Egypt joining their intention to ours as we opened ourselves to the flow of unconditional love.

Each of the four Archangels, accompanied by one of the Templar knights, positioned themselves at the four cardinal points of the Old City and, in answer to the highest call of our souls, held open the portals of all the realms of the heavens. Uriel and Richard were to the west, Gabriel and Edmund to the south, Raphael and Henry to the north, and to the east, at the Golden Gate, Michael and St Thomas prepared to stand vigil with us to await the dawn and the return of the Shekinah.

*****

We returned to the Mount of Olives and the Shrine of the Ascension in the quiet hours before dawn, bringing red and white roses with us to symbolize the sacred communion of male and female and the birthing of the cosmic child. We laid a rose of each colour and scattered petals at the shrine's gate before beginning the walk to the Golden Gate.

But before we did, Rebecca had been inspired to bring a phial of the essential oil spikenard to anoint our feet. Feeling as though we had been energetically given wings, by just after 4 a.m. we reached the lower slope of the Mount and, to our wonder, the Church of the Virgin Mary was already open at this early hour.

This Templar church commemorates the location of Mary's traditional place of rest. Now it was empty but for her presence.

The four of us walked down its ancient steps. And in the gentle quiet of Mary's inner sanctum, we laid another pair of roses, their stems free of thorns, and scattered petals before once more energizing our intentions for re-soulution.

*****

Emerging, we saw above us the Golden Gate of the Old City awaiting our arrival. And as we slowly continued on our way, great numbers of Moslem pilgrims spilled out onto the streets as they completed their overnight prayers on Temple Mount.

Wherever we had gone in the Old City, we had been aware of the ebb and flow of tensions between the faiths. And while no one was aggressive, we could sense many silently asking why we non-Moslems were here.

Cemeteries where the dead of the three faiths repose fill the valley between the Old City and the lower slopes of the Mount of Olives. As we walked the final part of our way to the Golden Gate, our path took us through the Moslem cemetery. Gazing back to the Mount, we saw the waning crescent of the Moon's final phase, a symbol of Islam, suspended low in the sky.

The Gate now loomed above us, but an iron fence denied access to it. As we climbed the last few yards, I reconciled myself to this being as close as we would physically approach.

People were now beginning to walk along the path beneath us. And a group of teenage boys, clearly angry and not understanding our presence here, shouted threateningly at us to leave.

While not wishing to cause an incident, we nonetheless were not prepared to give up in the face of this challenge. Our resolve held and the boys moved on, only for a second group, wielding sticks, to come along. This time, their shouts were less angry, more a final test that was prepared to concede the rights of everyone to be there. And eventually they too moved on.

The Elohim had guided me that the Shekinah would energetically return as the first rays of the dawn Sun reached the Gate. But as we continued to face east, waiting for the sunrise and more and more aware of our visibility, like a bride she appeared to be reluctant to show herself until the perfect moment.

Without thinking, I now glanced to my right and could not believe my eyes. There, previously unnoticed, was a gate in the iron fence that had held us away from the Golden Gate itself – and that gate was open!

*****

We now stood on the messiah line with our backs directly against the Golden Gate, awaiting the first rays of the Sun.

A young boy, the first beggar we had seen, walked slowly towards us. Coming through the gate in the fence, without a word he opened his hand for alms. Tony gave him all the shekels he had in his pocket and the boy turned to walk away.

As he did, I cried out for him to wait and he came towards me. All I had to offer him was my love and the few rose petals I still carried. Reaching out to each other I placed the petals in his hand. He looked down and then carefully placed his other palm over the petals, smiling gently at me. As he walked away and out of sight, we could see that he continued to hold the petals cupped safely in his hands as though they were the most precious of gifts.

Ahead of us, the summit of the Mount of Olives now became an intense beacon of translucent light, the bridal gown of the Shekinah a band of pure whiteness almost too bright to bear.

As the Sun finally rose majestically into sight, its first rays heralding her return, the transcendence of the Shekinah entered through the Gate, the bride returning to her bridegroom to reconsummate the sacred marriage of the Cosmos.

*****

The Old City was beginning to stir as we made our way back.

After the long night we were hoping to find some reviving coffee, but at this early hour there was nowhere open.

As we turned the corner, we saw ahead of us the group of boys who had wielded the sticks and shouted at us at the Gate. They clearly recognized us and there was nothing to do other than to take a deep breath and walk towards and past them.

But as we approached, one of them asked us, 'Would you like a coffee?'

As we grinned our thanks, they ushered us to the seats they had occupied at the side of the narrow street and while one went to organize coffee, the others began to chat.

In limited English, the burning question the previously most aggressive of the boys wanted to ask me was, what was my favourite film! Without answering, I asked via the boy who was translating for us, what was his favourite film?

Without hesitation he said, '*The Lord of the Rings.*'

Mine too!

*****

The guidance of the Elohim was for us to complete our work of re-soulution at the ancient site of Megiddo. There, the four-millennia-old high altar of the Canaanites was dedicated to the worship of El Shaddei. This sanctuary of the biblical YHWH overlooks the plain of Jezreel – the biblical Armageddon – the prophesied location of the final conflict between good and evil.

Excavations of the ruins have reconstructed the great altar that overlooks the plain below. While my three friends acted as sentries, I slowly walked towards the round man-high monument, journeying back four millennia to the seed-point of the ancient schism.

As I laid our final white rose at the base of the altar, I saw a flight of stairs leading up to its platform. Making my way to the very centre, I took a final step and, turning to face the plain of Armageddon, I scattered the rose petals of peace on its ancient stones.

Gazing across the vast plain, I closed my eyes and in my inner vision I now saw not the biblical prophesy of the final battle between good and evil but a great congress of peoples assembled from every nation and faith. This was an apocalypse of peace, the revelation of the Heaven on Mother Earth that we can co-create together.

As I returned to my companions and we came together, a butterfly, the beautiful symbol of metamorphosis, flew in front of us and alighted on the ground. We suddenly realized, though, that this was not a single butterfly but two conjoined in the act of mating – the perfect symbol of marital and cosmic bliss.

In this high place, we knew that YHWH now had what He wanted.

*****

Several days after returning home, still integrating my experiences, I received an e-mail from Sarah. Although it had been many months – in fact before Tony and I had left for Turkey – since I had heard of the plight of her son Isaac, they had both been in my prayers many times.

She had no knowledge of the journey we had undertaken, its timing or its culmination. Her e-mail simply said that Isaac's treatment is complete and that he is recovering well.

WALK ON!

As together we travel the path towards 2012 we each have, through our personal choices, the opportunity to act as midwife for Heaven on Mother Earth.

The greater empowerment we have available to us, however, is to actively co-create the path and from seed-points of hope and proactive intention to envisage a new way of loving and living together in peace, truth and justice.

Our journeys showed us time and time again how the extraordinary arises from and is validated by the ordinary. And how the extraordinary is ever-present in the ordinary. If we are willing to have eyes to see and ears to hear the subtle – and sometimes not-so-subtle – messages of our higher guidance, every one of us can realize that we are a soular hero.

In the words of Gautama Buddha, 'You cannot travel the path until you have become the Path itself.'

As each us makes our ongoing choices to become part of the Path to our cosmic destiny, we may also remember the Buddha's last words to his disciples:

'Walk on!'

卍 ॐ 卍

ABOUT THE AUTHOR

Jude Currivan is a healer and scientist who has studied consciousness and perennial wisdom teachings since childhood. She has a master's degree in physics specialising in cosmology and quantum physics, and a Ph.D. in archaeology, researching ancient cosmologies. Jude is a sensitive who has directly experienced multidimensional realities and worked with higher guidance all her life.

During a highly successful international business career that culminated in her being the Group Finance Director of two major international corporations, she obtained extensive experience in merging her intuitive gifts into a practical and well-grounded approach for managing organisational and cultural change.

Moving on from the corporate world in the mid-1990s, Jude brings her life-long experience and understanding to support the raising of awareness and sustainable healing and wholeness on personal and collective levels. Her pioneering work combines leading-edge science, consciousness research and spiritual wisdom into an empowering and inspiring worldview of integral reality. Her first book, *The Wave*, was published in 2005, and her second, *The 8th Chakra*, by Hay House in 2006.

For further information on Jude's work and details of how to contact her, please visit **www.judecurrivan.com**.

❊ ❊ ❊

We hope you enjoyed this Hay House book.
If you'd like to receive a free catalog featuring additional
Hay House books and products, or if you'd like information about the
Hay Foundation, please contact:

Hay House, Inc.
P.O. Box 5100
Carlsbad, CA 92018-5100

(760) 431-7695 or (800) 654-5126
(760) 431-6948 (fax) or (800) 650-5115 (fax)
www.hayhouse.com® • www.hayfoundation.org

❊ ❊ ❊

Published and distributed in Australia by:
Hay House Australia Pty. Ltd., 18/36 Ralph St., Alexandria NSW 2015
Phone: 612-9669-4299 • *Fax:* 612-9669-4144 • www.hayhouse.com.au

Published and distributed in the United Kingdom by:
Hay House UK, Ltd., 292B Kensal Rd., London W10 5BE • *Phone:*
44-20-8962-1230 • *Fax:* 44-20-8962-1239 • www.hayhouse.co.uk

Published and distributed in the Republic of South Africa by:
Hay House SA (Pty), Ltd., P.O. Box 990, Witkoppen 2068 • *Phone/Fax:*
27-11-467-8904 • orders@psdprom.co.za • www.hayhouse.co.za

Published in India by:
Hay House Publishers India, Muskaan Complex, Plot No. 3, B-2,
Vasant Kunj, New Delhi 110 070 • *Phone:* 91-11-4176-1620
Fax: 91-11-4176-1630 • www.hayhouse.co.in

Distributed in Canada by:
Raincoast, 9050 Shaughnessy St., Vancouver, B.C. V6P 6E5
Phone: (604) 323-7100 • *Fax:* (604) 323-2600 • www.raincoast.com

❊ ❊ ❊

Tune in to **HayHouseRadio.com®** for the best in inspirational
talk radio featuring top Hay House authors!
And, sign up via the Hay House USA Website to receive the Hay House online
newsletter and stay informed about what's going on with your favorite authors.
You'll receive bimonthly announcements about Discounts and Offers,
Special Events, Product Highlights, Free Excerpts, Giveaways, and more!
www.hayhouse.com®